TEACHING TOWARD DEMOCRACY

WITHDRAWN

TEACHER'S TOOLKIT SERIES

1

Teaching for Success:
Developing Your Teacher Identity in Today's Classroom
Brad Olsen (UC–Santa Cruz)

2

Teaching English Learners:
Fostering Language and the Democratic Experience
Kip Téllez (UC–Santa Cruz)

3

Teaching Without Bells: What We Can Learn
from Powerful Practice in Small Schools
Joey Feldman (New Haven Unified School District)

4

Leading from the Inside Out:
Expanded Roles for Teachers in Equitable Schools
W. Norton Grubb and Lynda Tredway
(UC–Berkeley)

5

Teaching Toward Democracy:
Educators as Agents of Change
William Ayers (U of Ill–Chicago), Kevin Kumashiro (U of Ill–Chicago),
Erica Meiners (Northeastern Illinois University),
Therese Quinn (The Art Institute of Chicago), and David Stovall (U of Ill–Chicago)

6

Making a Difference:
Developing Meaningful Careers in Education
Karen Hunter Quartz (UCLA), Brad Olsen (UC–Santa Cruz),
Lauren Anderson (UCLA), and Kimberly Barraza Lyons (UCLA)

TEACHING TOWARD DEMOCRACY

Educators as Agents of Change

William Ayers, Kevin Kumashiro,
Erica Meiners, Therese Quinn, and David Stovall

TEACHER'S TOOLKIT SERIES

Paradigm Publishers
Boulder • London

KH

Lucille Clifton, "poem in praise of menstruation" and excerpt from "wishes for sons" from *Quilting: Poems 1987–1990*. Copyright 1991 by Lucille Clifton. Reprinted with the permission of BOA Editions, Ltd., www.boaeditions.org.

"homage to my hips" Copyright 1980 by Lucille Clifton first appeared in *Two-Headed Woman*, published by University of Massachusetts Press. Now appears in *Good Woman: Poems and a Memoir 1969–1980*, published by Boa Editions. Reprinted by permission of Curtis Brown Ltd.

Copyright © 2010 Paradigm Publishers

Published in the United States by Paradigm Publishers, 2845 Wilderness Place, Suite 200, Boulder, CO 80301 USA.

Paradigm Publishers is the trade name of Birkenkamp & Company, LLC, Dean Birkenkamp, President and Publisher.

Library of Congress Cataloging-in-Publication Data

Teaching toward democracy : educators as agents of change /
William Ayers . . . [et al.].
    p. cm. — (Teacher's toolkit series)
    Includes bibliographical references and index.
    ISBN 978-1-59451-843-0 (pbk. : alk. paper)
    1. Citizenship—Study and teaching—United States.   2. Teaching—Social aspects—United States.   3. Democracy and education—United States.   4. Social change—United States.   I. Ayers, William, 1944–
    LC1091.T428 2010
    370.11'5—dc22

                                            2009043472

Printed and bound in the United States of America on acid-free paper that meets the standards of the American National Standard for Permanence of Paper for Printed Library Materials.

Design by Cindy Young.

14 13 12 11 10   1 2 3 4 5

9/2/11

CONTENTS

SERIES FOREWORD

THIS TEACHER'S TOOLKIT series is a set of six related books written for prospective, new, and experienced teachers who are committed to students and families, who conceive of themselves as agents of democratic change, and who are eager to think more deeply, more broadly, and more practically about their work in education. All six books succinctly link theory with practice, present extended arguments for improving education, and wrap their discussions around successful examples of the topics in question.

Although each book is its own resource, the books in the Toolkit series share some common views about teaching. For one, all of the books treat teachers not as mere deliverers of curriculum but as active, three-dimensional professionals capable of diagnosing student learning, developing powerful educational experiences, assessing and adjusting student learning, and forming productive relationships with children and adults in schools. Another view all of the books share is that teaching is hard work that is among the most important kinds of work any society requires. My grandmother used to say that no society can survive without farmers or teachers. I think that is still true. Teaching is undeniably difficult work, but it is also frequently enjoyable work because it is so challenging, meaningful, and success oriented. These books are for teachers who have accepted the challenges of teaching because they relish the satisfaction of the work, they enjoy helping young people grow, and they know that quality education is necessary for the health of our world.

A third commonality about teaching among these books is their shared presumption that teachers are always looking for ways to improve. Teaching is a profession in which one enters as a novice, develops expertise over time, and continues to grow and change throughout the whole of one's career. The Toolkit books are written for teachers at multiple points in their career cycle: Beginning teachers will learn new ways to think about learning, students, and about what it means to become a successful educator. Early- and middle-career teachers can reflect on their own practice in light of the ideas, strategies, and stories of these books—and they can use the books to deepen and broaden their future work. Veteran teachers can see themselves and their varied experiences inside the perspectives of the books, as well as figure out how they can continue to challenge themselves and their students—and perhaps take on other kinds of education work such as mentoring newer teachers, advocating for students on a broader stage, or writing about their own teaching. No matter where readers are in their education careers, these books offer powerful learning and useful opportunities for professional reflection.

The six books are sequenced to loosely follow both the career cycle of teaching and the fact that, as teachers progress, they often widen their sphere of influence. Book 1 in the series is *Teaching for Success: Developing Your Teacher Identity in Today's Classroom*, by Brad Olsen. This book focuses on the processes of "becoming a teacher" and explores how to teach well in this contemporary age. Wrapping its conversations about teacher development around the core concept of teacher identity, the book offers its own teacher learning experience: how to recognize, adjust, and maximize the many ways your personal self and your professional self become integrated in your teaching work.

Book 2, *Teaching English Learners: Fostering Language and the Democratic Experience*, by Kip Téllez, focuses on what teachers can do in their classrooms in order to better understand and more effectively teach English learners. Drawing from research and experience not only on learning and teaching but also on culture, language, immigration, and contemporary politics, Téllez offers a unique guide for use by U.S. teachers interested in deeply and compassionately supporting the growth of students whose native language is not English.

Book 3 in the series is *Teaching Without Bells: What We Can Learn from Powerful Instruction in Small Schools*, by Joey Feldman. This book offers a valuable look at how teaching and learning are fundamentally influenced by school size. The book's premise is that student and teacher experiences in education are direct functions of their school's size (and its accompanying influence on how schools are organized). Focusing on challenges and benefits of teaching in small high schools, Feldman's book helps readers consider where they might want to teach and—no matter the size of their school site—how they can teach well by maximizing lessons from the small schools movement.

Book 4, *Leading from the Inside Out: Expanded Roles for Teachers in Equitable Schools*, by Norton Grubb and Lynda Tredway, opens up the professional world of the teacher by offering new ways to think about school reform from the vantage point of the teacher. The authors make a compelling case for teachers as the key ingredient in education reform and schools as the lever for democratic educational change. Presenting a blueprint for a new kind of school in which teachers are not only classroom instructors but education reformers as well, Grubb and Tredway illustrate why we have the schools we have today and how broad-minded teachers can transform them into successful schools for tomorrow.

Book 5, *Teaching Toward Democracy: Educators as Agents of Change*, by William Ayers, Kevin Kumashiro, Erica Meiners, Therese Quinn, and David Stovall, also considers teachers as agents of change on a broader scale. The authors share their ideas about how teachers can better humanize schooling for students, combat some of the current failings of market models of education, and extend their teaching work past the school day and outside the school walls. Their book invites readers into a view of education seen through the eyes of students, and it provides thoughtful strategies to enact teaching for social justice as not just a popular slogan but as an authentic focus on human rights and social equity for all.

And, to close out the series, Book 6, *Making a Difference: Developing Meaningful Careers in Education*, by Karen Hunter Quartz, Brad Olsen, Lauren Anderson, and Kimberly Barraza Lyons, looks at whole careers in education. This book examines the dynamic lives and work of several educators in Los Angeles and investigates why teachers stay in the classroom or shift to other kinds of education roles, such as school administrator, curriculum coordinator, or teacher mentor. The book unpacks the sometimes maddening complexity of the teaching profession and offers a roadmap for how teachers can, themselves, re-main challenged and satisfied as educators without relaxing their com-mitments to students.

There are different approaches to reading the books in this series. One way is to consider the whole series as a coherent set of sequenced conversations about teaching. In this manner, you might read the books one at a time, all the way through, inserting yourself into the text of the books: Do the stories and experiences in the books ring true for you? How will you use these books to improve your practice, broaden your influence, and deepen your professional satisfaction? You might imag-ine, as you read the books this way, that you are sitting in a room with the authors—listening to their ideas, questioning them, actively engag-ing with their arguments, or talking back to the text when necessary.

Or perhaps you might use these books as textbooks—as thoughtful primers on selected topics that interest you. In this manner, you might pick and choose particular chapters to study: Which specific ideas will you implement in your teaching tomorrow? Are there further readings or key resources that you will hunt down and look at on your own? What concrete activities will you try out? Write notes in the margins of the books and return to the chapters regularly. Photocopy single pages (not whole chapters, please!) to share with peers. Use the books as you plan lessons or design curricula. Engage with the reflection questions at the end of each book's chapters. You will find occasionally in the margins cross-references on specific topics to other books in the series. When you read "Cross-Reference, See Book 2 . . ." you can use the numbered list of titles on p. ii to correlate each reference to the in-tended book.

Or, you may pick some of the books to read collectively with other educators—maybe with your teacher education cohort, or as a group of teachers working with a mentor, or perhaps as part of a teacher inquiry group that you set up with colleagues. Group discussion of these books allows their arguments, perspectives, and examples to prompt your own collective reflection and professional growth: What themes from the books call out to you? What points might you disagree with? How might different educators among you interpret parts of these books in different, perhaps competing, ways? How can these books inspire you to create specific collaborative projects or teacher networks at your school site? You may find the reflection questions at the end of each chapter particularly useful for group conversation.

This series of books is called the "Teacher's Toolkit," but maybe, for some, the idea of a *toolkit* for teachers may not, at first glance, be apt. Picturing a toolkit could conjure images of a steel toolbox or super-hero belt full of hardware for educators—a diagnostic screwdriver, the clawhammer of homework, a set of precision wrenches for adjusting student learning on the fly. Such images are, well, just too instrumental. They risk suggesting that teaching is mechanical or automatic, or that what good educators do is select utensils from their box to apply when needed. That doesn't describe the kind of teaching I know and love. It erroneously suggests that students are to be fastened with bolts or hammered into obedience, or that learning is gut-wrenchingly rigid. And, to my mind, such a view treats teachers as technicians trained by rote, using tools given to them by others, following directions written on the outside of the box.

Instead, the authors of these books conceive of education as less fixed, more fluid, less finished, more uncertain, and certainly far more complicated than anything for which traditional tools would work. These authors—based on their own years of experience as classroom teachers, educational researchers, school administrators, and university professors—view education similarly to educational philosopher John Dewey when, in 1934, he wrote:

> About 40 years ago, a new idea dawned in education. Educators began to see that education should parallel life, that the school should reproduce the child's world. In this new type of education the child, instead of the curriculum, became the centre of interest, and since the child is active, changing, creative—education ceased to be static, [and] became dynamic and creative in response to the needs of the child.[1]

Like Dewey, I understand teaching and learning to be context-specific, highly creative, dynamically student-centered activities that are as complicated and multifaceted as life itself. And just as important.

So let's reimagine the analogy of a teacher's toolkit. A *toolkit* for teachers could instead be a metaphor for a thoughtful, useful, provocative bundle of perspectives, theories, and approaches for teachers—a set of lively teaching discussions written by different authors who share some common ground. This bundle would empathize with teachers since its authors are all teachers, as well as education researchers and writers: they know both how difficult and how rewarding teaching can be. But it would also exhort teachers not to fall down on the job—not to shirk their work, make excuses, or lessen their resolve to support students.

The bundle of teaching conversations could share stories from the classroom that reveal teaching to be kaleidoscopic: made up of thousands of shifting views, hundreds of competing relations, and dozens of different ways to succeed with children. The stories would reveal how to be a great teacher and why doing so is so damned important. The bundle of ideas and perspectives would include actual examples of good teaching, lesson ideas, and lots of research tidbits useful for prospective and practicing educators. Yes, that could be a toolkit I would want to own. It would be a kit full of thoughtful perspectives, research summaries, wisdom of practice, and impassioned words of advice from handpicked educationalists. An "idea kit," really. A boxed set of thoughtful primers on how to teach well for social change in the current global climate.

John Dewey famously built binaries in his writing—teaching is either this or that; students learn in this way but not in that way—only to collapse the binary in the end and suggest that education is too complicated for easy contradictions. So I'll take a page from Dewey's playbook and attempt the same. Maybe we can consider this book series as not an either/or. Not as *either* a box of teaching instruments *or* a collection of thoughtful conversations about education, but as both: a set of tangible strategies for teachers to make their own and a loosely bundled collection of professional arguments for use by educators in order to think for themselves, but in deeper and newer ways than before. That's the way that I prefer to envision this teacher's toolkit.

No matter how you choose to make use of the books in the Teacher's Toolkit, it is our sincere hope that you will find value in them. We have tried to make them accessible, conversational, substantive, and succinct. We all believe that teaching is a fundamentally important profession, and, if this world is to improve and grow, it will be because our teachers can help future generations in becoming wise, creative, and critical thinkers who put their ideas into action toward improving the societies they will inherit. You are an essential part of that human process.

—Brad Olsen
University of California, Santa Cruz

NOTE

1. John Dewey, "Tomorrow May Be Too Late: Save the Schools Now." Reprinted in J. Boydston (ed.), *John Dewey: The Later Works, 1925–1953, Vol. 9: 1933–1934* (Carbondale: Southern Illinois University Press, 1986), 386.

INTRODUCTION

CHARLES DICKENS published *Hard Times* in London in 1854, over 150 years ago. In the opening paragraphs, he describes with raging fidelity the first harsh lesson drummed into the heads of unsuspecting new teachers:

> "Now, what I want is, Facts. Teach these boys and girls nothing but Facts. Facts alone are wanted in life. Plant nothing else, and root out everything else. You can only form the minds of reasoning animals upon Facts: nothing else will ever be of any service to them. This is the principle on which I bring up my own children, and this is the principle on which I bring up these children. Stick to Facts, Sir!" . . .
>
> The speaker, and the schoolmaster . . . swept with their eyes the inclined plane of little vessels then and there arranged in order, ready to have imperial gallons of facts poured into them until they were full to the brim.

This fraught description of nineteenth-century English schooling sounds weirdly resonant, curiously close at hand, quite a lot like the school world we teachers face right here, right now. One would think that education and schooling in a modern contemporary democracy would look remarkably different from the tyrannical classrooms of Great Britain under the rule of Queen Victoria. Monarchies, after all, demand fealty first and foremost, whereas democracies, at least theoretically, are built on the active engagement and participation of a free and enlightened people. And because schools—no matter where or when—are always a mirror and window into whatever social order created and sustains them, we can easily imagine the society that the above-mentioned "imperial gallons of facts" are meant to sustain and reproduce; what's harder to reconcile is the oddly familiar feeling of that autocratic classroom picture—and the brute logic behind it—in our own democratic society and our modern classroom contexts.

Key concept
A democracy is a form of associative living in which people make the decisions that affect their lives.

This book examines the contested space of schooling in a **democracy** with a focus on the unique challenges and abiding opportunities that teaching in a democratic society provides. We discuss the qualities of mind as well as the practical arts that teachers might explore and work to develop as they become more effective educators. Some chapters open with an entirely expected feature in the lives of teachers in schools (working with parents and communities, for example, or dealing with classroom discipline and management) and attempt, then, to illuminate that commonplace in new, helpful, and—we hope—startling ways; others present possible interventions any teacher might make in any classroom—for example, using the arts as an organizing center and metaphor for teaching more generally, or rethinking the press of politics on our everyday practice. We do this by foregrounding the central theme of the book: the democratic ideal as a necessary starting point and context in which to enact our teaching.

Each chapter offers examples of individuals grappling with problems and thinking out loud as they do so, providing—we hope—not so much a model to copy or clone as an instance of teaching as a kind of reflection-in-action, something that may prove to be a useful approach for people rethinking or initiating their work as teachers in classrooms. Each chapter builds on and depends on the others—from teachers and classrooms to whole schools and community engagement to educational policy—and woven together they come closer to a kind of life in classrooms that lives up to our democratic dreams and our highest aspirations for what teaching and schooling might yet become.

You are already the experts on your own lives, and you will very soon be the experts on your own teaching.

This is written in the spirit of notes, conversations, and letters we wish we'd gotten from mentors and guides when we were starting on our own journeys into teaching. We do not pretend to know it all—or much of anything at all—and we are not assuming the patronizing posture of people who think that their own precious experiences are the center of the universe. You are already the experts on your own lives, and you will very soon be the experts on your own teaching; we simply want to look with you at some of the possibilities and the obstacles, our shared ideals and the rough realities, classrooms as they are and classrooms as they might be.

We intend here to upend received wisdom and disrupt the dogma of common sense through the presentation of practical examples, evidence and argument, and pointed questions designed not so much to answer in any definitive way the challenges we present, but rather to provoke further reflection and deeper reconsideration. We hope to add to the repertoire of skills teachers can access as they make their twisty ways into teaching for democracy, and we invite readers, moreover, to reexamine their own thinking, have confidence in their own higher aspirations and larger purposes, find important allies, and locate themselves more confidently in the noble tradition of teaching as democratic work.

The process of writing this book together—a book with five authors, like a soup with five cooks or a cabin with five carpenters—has been, as you might imagine, challenging. We have much broad agreement on the big issues of democracy and education, of course, or we never would have undertaken this project together in the first place; we also come from diverse experiences and standpoints, different perspectives and approaches, distinct styles and modes of expression. We know one another well enough through our shared work on school improvement and community social justice projects, but some of us embrace a more scholarly approach while others of us begin in a more activist place. All of us return again and again to classrooms and local communities as essential sites in which to enact and realize our democratic ambitions.

We thought long and hard about creating an edited book made up of single-authored chapters; we decided in the end that our process was worthwhile as an exercise in a more collaborative way of being, an improvisational and collective approach that more closely mirrors the way each of us experiences teaching and tries to carry out our community work. We chose not to name which one of us put which words on which page, which of us edited and challenged this or that formulation, or where the inevitable compromises are located. The result is a book with some rough edges—please be forewarned, and we apologize in advance—jarring transitions, and (we hope) intriguing style shifts, but a book nonetheless infused with the feel and the experience of an intentional temporary community.

Because of the occasional sharp shifts in voice and content, we suggest that you read a chapter and then clean the refrigerator, read another and go to the gym, read a bit more and take a walk. The choppy spots may become less cause for alarm and point instead to the unfinished, drafty, and incomplete nature of the work at hand: we are—each of us—works in progress lurching forward in a dynamic and contingent world. This is a metaphor, then, for teaching itself.

The five of us are teachers and professors now, and we are all intrepid scribblers trying to capture on the page—

drafting, editing, redrafting—our abiding desire to participate in making a more balanced world. One of us teaches in high school, one works in a reentry school for ex-prisoners, one directs a human rights organization, one is a street poet, and one is a performance artist.

We are all Chicagoans now as well, and we each find in Chicago a unique set of challenges and circumstances; it is a city where chaos and opportunity contend and embrace in what seems an endlessly refreshing and often exhausting dance of the dialectic. Chicago, seen through another lens, can be considered not singular at all, but rather a somewhat representative site of the complex and abiding crises experienced by people everywhere, particularly in poor areas and in communities of color: deindustrialization and a lack of viable job opportunities; massive un- and underemployment; gentrification and "urban removal"; a runaway prison-industrial complex, militarization, and surveillance; and galloping environmental degradation.

Chicago, of course, is not and can never be a single thing, the same for all people at all times. The city of Chicago means different things, depending on the situation and circumstance, author or speaker, standpoint and perspective. Even the word *city* has endless colors and shades—in certain contexts, *city* is racially coded ("city schools," "inner-city," "city hospital"); in another context, it's a class signifier (the city opera, the city center). The city is so many things at once, colliding, overlapping, and contradicting. Exploring the physical shapes of Chicago can be thrilling in itself, but the real excitement for us exists in excavating the fault lines of culture and history, of education and politics, and then asking ourselves what we intend to *do* about any of it.

Nelson Algren wrote of city politics in his famous love poem to our shared home, *Chicago: City on the Make:*

Not that there's been any lack of honest men and women sweating out Jane Addams' hopes here—but they get only two outs to the inning while the hustlers are taking four. When Big Bill Thompson put in the fix for Capone he tied the town to the rackets for keeps.

So that when the reform mayor who followed him attempted to enforce the Prohibition laws, he wakened such warfare on the streets that the Do-Gooders themselves put Thompson back at the wheel, realizing that henceforward nobody but an outlaw could maintain a semblance of law and order on the common highway. Big Bill greeted his fellow citizens correctly then with a cheery, "Fellow hoodlums!"

The best any mayor could do with the city since is just keep it in repair.

Yet the Do-Gooders still go doggedly forward making the hustlers struggle for their gold week in and week out, year after year, once or twice a decade tossing an unholy fright into the boys. And since it's a ninth-inning town, the ball game never being over till the last man is out, it remains Jane Addams' town as well as Big Bill's. The ball game isn't over yet.

Over a century ago, when Jane Addams established Hull House—a place that still exists, and a site where the five of us interact with one another regularly—she argued that building communities of care and compassion required more than "doing good," more than volunteerism, more than the beneficent but ultimately controlling stance of a Lady Bountiful. It required, rather, a radical oneness with others in distress. She had this in mind when she opened her settlement house and lived there with families of crisis and need, saw the world through their eyes, and in fighting for their humanity fought as well for her own.

There are today countless men and women—and we count ourselves among them—sweating out Jane Addams's hopes here, naming situations and circumstances as unacceptable, working to repair deficiencies and to right wrongs. These men and women think of themselves as acting *in solidarity with*—rather than *in service to*—the people with whom they work. That distinction is enormous, and we will return to it again and again.

Contemporary Chicago enjoys another noteworthy distinction: it's home to President Barack Obama. "Yes, We Can," he'd proclaimed throughout the campaign, and his election as the first black president signaled the promise of change, of progress, of hope. The fact that he'd been a community organizer for many years on Chicago's storied South Side, and that he had within his experience and knowledge the realities of that particular life on the ground, fueled a sea of rising expectations. During the heat of the primary battle, when asked which candidate he thought Martin Luther King Jr. would support, Senator Obama responded without hesitation— Reverend King would not likely endorse any of us, he said, because he'd be in the streets building a movement for justice. That's a community organizer's answer— President Obama understands power at the top; he has also experienced power in the neighborhood, the community, the shop or the factory, the school and the street. We might keep that idea foremost in our consciousness going forward, for it underlines the fact that *in a democracy we don't wait passively wondering what the king has in mind for his subjects; the people themselves are sovereign, we are the collective power, and we all have the opportunity and the responsibility to open our eyes, pay attention, and get busy.*

Focus point

In January 2009, activist-educators reflected in online discussion groups about the prospects for the new administration, and the question again and again was "Yes, we can . . . what?" The dominant tone of hope was mixed with feelings of deep concern, particularly for our nation's youth. There was much discussion about the danger that, for all its promise, this administration, like so many before it, could come to ruin in the furnaces of war.

Within weeks of his election President Obama began to nominate members to his cabinet: warriors at the

Pentagon, of course, but also old-line hacks at State and in the White House were handed the portfolios to rescue the economy—foxes guarding the chicken house for sure. The new secretary of education would be Arne Duncan, and his Senate confirmation hearings brought a chorus of praise for his accomplishments over the past seven years as CEO of the Chicago Public Schools.

Duncan's work in Chicago strongly suggested the direction in which he would take the nation's public schools. His signature initiative, Renaissance 2010, launched in 2004 with the aim to open one hundred new smaller schools and close or "turn around" so-called failing schools. As of this writing, seventy-five new schools have opened, many of them charter schools that serve far fewer students from low-income families and fewer students with disabilities or limited English-language proficiency than regular neighborhood public schools. More than a third of them are in communities that are not high-needs areas.

Perhaps most important, nothing in these moves focuses on supporting teachers' work over the long haul, engaging parents and communities in the education of their children, offering an intellectually rich curriculum, or fighting for equity and the generous resourcing of needy schools. So for all the fanfare and the hoopla, the heart and the soul of the matter is missing.

During Duncan's tenure, district-wide high school test scores did not go up, dropout rates continued apace, and most of the lowest-performing high schools saw scores drop. The evidence was clear: the cheery media accounts notwithstanding, Renaissance 2010 was failing to live up to its elaborate public relations claims and was doing little or nothing to support those students who struggled most.

The blueprint for Renaissance 2010 lies in a 2003 report by the Commercial Club of Chicago, "Left Behind," which mapped out a strategy for schools to align more closely with the goals and needs of the business elite.

Central to that strategy was the creation of new charter schools managed by for-profit businesses and operated outside the framework of parent-led, elected local school councils and teacher unions—groups that historically have put the welfare of poor and minority students before that of the business sector.

Business leaders have long influenced America's public schools. In the early 1900s, the business sector influenced how large school districts were consolidated and managed, and a century later the Business Roundtable (which currently consists of the top 300 business CEOs in the United States) influenced how policymakers defined "standards" and "accountability." Today public debates are framed by business principles, and certain of these assumptions go unquestioned and underanalyzed, considered to be simply "**common sense.**" This includes the assumption that improvement comes when schools are put into competition with one another, like businesses in a so-called free market.

Key concept
Common sense is
what we take for
granted as the
way things are
and/or should be.

Duncan's initiatives were steeped in a free-market model of reform, particularly the notion that school choice and new charter and specialty schools would motivate educators to work harder and do better, as would penalties for not meeting standards. But neither research nor practice supports these conclusions. There is, instead, evidence that opening new schools outside the public system—that is, without the initiative or cooperation of teachers and parents—and encouraging choice and competition will not raise achievement throughout the district. Charter schools in particular are not outperforming regular schools. There is evidence that choice programs actually exacerbate racial segregation. And there is evidence that high-stakes testing actually increases the already dismal and entirely unacceptable dropout rate.

Cross-Reference
For more on the
policies and
effects of
charter schools,
see Book 4,
Chapter I.

What's significant here is that Duncan's efforts exemplified a much larger movement to radically change, largely dismantle, and privatize public schools in the

United States—a movement driven for the past few decades by a varied collection of probusiness, conservative, neoliberal, and fundamentalist organizations. This movement has put forward a range of seemingly disparate but ideologically coherent policy initiatives, such as

- the privatizing of various educational services and functions in ways that profit the business sector and leave little accountability for elected officials;
- the expansion of school-choice and school-voucher programs that divert funding from the schools in most need;
- the creation of alternative, fast-track teacher and administrator certification programs that put educators with less preparation in schools with the greatest need;
- the adoption of policies that hinder labor organizing and the involvement of local communities in school governance, groups that have historically advocated for underserved students;
- the implementation of high-stakes testing with punitive results for students and schools, placing blame for failure on individual effort while ignoring such institutional and structural factors as inequitable funding;
- the narrowing of curriculum and learning standards and outcomes, privileging only certain perspectives and learning styles;
- the incorporation of the military and fundamentalist Christianity into public schools.

Focus point   *One way that the movement to dismantle public education has been successful at changing education policy is through strategic messages that influence or* frame *what the general public takes to be "common sense" about what schools should look like and how schools should be reformed.* In fact, this movement has become so successful at framing the debate as to influence even those who have historically been associated with fierce and persistent advocacy for public education, resulting in initiatives—such as those regarding school safety and closing achievement gaps—by "liberal" organizations that indirectly serve contradictory purposes. Arne Duncan's appointment as secretary of education signals the extent to which the Obama administration is in the thrall of narrow and counterproductive framings of education reform.

"Standards" is one frame that is now embraced by groups that have historically opposed one another on education policy issues. In January 2002, President George W. Bush signed into law No Child Left Behind (NCLB), which reauthorized the Elementary and Secondary Education Act and instituted changes that both Democrats and Republicans were calling the most substantial since the law's creation in 1965. Although claimed by the Bush administration, NCLB had wide bipartisan support and was cosponsored by one of the more senior and liberal members of the Democratic Party, Senator Edward Kennedy.

But NCLB did not originate with the Bush administration; much of the framework for NCLB was developed in the final years of the Clinton administration under Democratic appointees and staff. Although some of the details of NCLB shifted with the change of administration, several central concepts or dominant frames remained intact. In fact, in the presidential campaigns of subsequent Democratic candidates (Al Gore in 2000, John Kerry in 2004, and Barack Obama in 2008), the public heard proposals that may have differed in the details but remained firmly within four central frames:

1. *Standards:* We need to have high standards for students, teachers, and schools, as determined only by certain groups in society.

2. *Accountability:* We need to hold students, teachers, and schools accountable for reaching those standards and demonstrating that they did so based on standardized tests.

**Any reform
enacted on the
backs of
teachers is
doomed to fail;
any reform that
discounts the
experiences and
wisdom of
teachers and
parents will be
stillborn.**

3. *Sanctions:* There will be sanctions and punishments meted out for not meeting those standards, and rewards for doing so.

4. *Choice:* In those schools that do not meet standards, parents should have the choice to move their children elsewhere.

The problems with all this are legion, starting with the fact that any reform enacted on the backs of teachers is doomed to fail; any reform that discounts the experiences and wisdom of teachers and parents will be stillborn. The many challenges highlighted in Chicago, but emanating outward to the nation, provide one context for us to understand the rising tide of mediocrity in educational reform and the importance of educators struggling together to get it right, and then organizing to speak up and speak out.

Teachers and parents tend to speak from the grassy grass roots and from the ground up. We speak from classrooms, homes, neighborhoods, barrios, reservations, cities and towns, and all kinds of diverse communities. And so we return to the wellspring of all of our efforts: this child, this student, this street, this school.

Focus point

Every issue and argument in this book, each example and story, is based on the idea that democracy is built on a particularly precious and fragile ideal: *every human being is of infinite and incalculable value, each a unique intellectual, emotional, physical, spiritual, moral, and creative force, each born free and equal in dignity and rights, endowed with reason and conscience, and deserving, then, a community of solidarity, a sense of brotherhood and sisterhood, recognition and respect.* We note, as well, that while children and their families are the root of our concern, any honest and moral accounting of the lives of our students sweeps us immediately into the wider world and opens our eyes to the grinding effects of poverty, the widening gap between the haves and the have-nots both here and around the globe, the horrors of war, and the gaping abyss of environmental catastrophe. We cannot pretend to be child-centered and at the same time bury our heads against the concentric circles of context that both shape our students' lives here and now and expose the possibilities and perils they will surely face in the future.

Respect for all persons—for teachers and students, for parents and community members—is a notable characteristic of good democratic schools. Consequently, democratic educators focus their efforts not on the production of things so much as on the full development of human beings who are capable of controlling and transforming their own lives, of engaged people who can participate actively in civic and public life, and who can think and act ethically in a complex and ever-changing world. Democratic teaching encourages students to develop initiative and imagination, the capacity to name the world, the wisdom to identify the obstacles to their full humanity and to the humanity of others, and the courage to act on whatever the known demands.

Revitalizing our classrooms and our communities based on the core democratic ideal that *every human being is of immeasurable worth, that each is the one and only who will ever trod the earth, that each deserves, simply by being born, unqualified respect* is critical work for teachers, and it has huge implications for curriculum and teaching, for what's taught and how. It points in the first place to the importance of opposing the hidden curriculum of obedience and conformity in favor of teaching things like initiative, questioning, investigation, doubt, skepticism, criticism, generosity, courage, imagination, and creativity—these are central and not peripheral to a democratic school experience. These are the qualities we must find ways to model and nourish, encourage and defend in our classrooms if democracy is going to become more than a few slogans and symbols, if it is to flourish and endure.

This belief in the preciousness and the infinite value of every human being shapes our work as teachers and as

Initiative, questioning, investigation, doubt, skepticism, criticism, generosity, courage, imagination, and creativity— these are central and not peripheral to a democratic school experience.

citizens of a democracy. It insists that we gear our efforts to helping every human being reach a fuller measure of his or her humanity. It invites people on a journey to become more thoughtful and more capable, more powerful and courageous, and more exquisitely alive in their projects and their pursuits. An unyielding belief in the unity of humanity—always revolutionary, and never more so than today—is never quite finished, forever in the process of being defined and reached for, and yet it is central to achieving a just society. Neither a commodity with readily recognized features nor a product for consumption, the democratic ideal is an aspiration to be continually nourished, engaged, and exercised—it is a dynamic, expansive experiment that must be achieved over and over again by every individual and each successive generation, if it is to live at all.

There is a powerful legacy of democratic education to uncover and embrace. This legacy comes to life in the same way that offspring find themselves in possession of an inheritance: as offspring, we are in a relationship and in conversation with our forebears no less than with one another. Lillian Weber and Eric Rofes, John Dewey and Paulo Freire, Barbara Biber and Viola Bernard, W. E. B. Du Bois and Fanny Jackson Coppin and Myles Horton, Amilcar Cabral and James Baldwin and bell hooks, Haywood Burns and Father Milani and Eqbal Ahmad, and Frantz Fanon and Edward Said and Ella Baker—democratic educators today can claim that rich and wildly diverse heritage, but as their "children" we also have responsibility to the present and the future. We honor our freedom-loving forebears by loving freedom in the present tense, and we will spend our inheritance, finally, as we see fit. All of us must decide for ourselves, individually and together, how we will go forward from here.

Focus point

Central to an education for citizenship, participation, engagement, and democracy is developing in students and teachers alike the ability to think for themselves, to question, to imagine alternatives. We must each develop a mind of our own; we can then find ways to join hands with others in order to act on our own judgments and in our own freedom. The way things are is not inevitable; human progress and freedom are always the result of thoughtful action. We must as teachers listen and speak, engage and witness.

Teachers ought to become aware of the stakes, aware as well that there is no simple technique or linear path that will take us where we need to go and then allow us to live out comfortable teaching lives, untroubled, settled, and finished. There is no promised land in teaching, just the aching and persistent tension between reality and possibility.

We teach toward democracy; we reach toward freedom; we crawl toward love.

FURTHER READING

1964 Mississippi Freedom School Curriculum. http://www.educationand democracy.org/ED_FSC.html.
A provocative example of teaching to change the world.

Delpit, Lisa. 2006. *Other People's Children: Cultural Conflict in the Classroom.* New York: New Press.
A revelation about how teaching about the culture of power can save your life.

Freire, Paulo. 1970/2000. *Pedagogy of the Oppressed.* New York: Continuum.
A generative work contrasting schooling as the passive acceptance of the status quo with education as the practice of freedom.

Gaines, Ernest. 2001. *A Lesson Before Dying.* London: Serpent's Tail.
A novel that evokes the life-and-death tensions of teaching for human dignity and freedom in an unjust world.

Valenzuela, Angela. 1999. *Subtractive Schooling: U.S.-Mexican Youth and the Politics of Caring.* Albany: State University of New York Press.
A powerful study of the negative effects of formal schooling on the education of kids.

CHAPTER ONE

OPENING THE CLASSROOM DOOR

- Building the Environment for Learning

- Atmosphere, Experience, Technique, Voice

- Creating a Democratic Culture

- Embracing Contradictions

- Finding the Wisdom in the Room

THERE'S SO MUCH to learn, so much to know and to do as we make our wobbly ways into teaching, that it can seem entirely overwhelming: "this can't be done," we hear ourselves saying over and over. That's an entirely common and natural feeling, and you're not alone. If you stick with it, break it down, and take it step by step, there can be an end to the tunnel where joy and light and even a little ecstasy live side by side with awe. Of course, the end of any particular tunnel is the beginning of other horizons and newer challenges; welcome to the dynamic world of the classroom.

Before we open our own classroom door, let's take a short voyage that just might shine a different kind of light on our experiences here and now.

On a recent evening in a small, poorly lit classroom high in the hills above Caracas, Venezuela, a literacy circle was under way: ten people had pulled their chairs close together—a young woman of perhaps age nineteen, a grandmother over sixty-five years old, two men in their forties—and were struggling to read. They were listening to each other's stories, offering commentary and suggestions for further elaboration, sometimes on the writing itself but as often on the content covered by the narrative.

"If the child is crying from a tooth coming," the older woman told the nineteen-year-old, who had read a two-sentence piece about staying up with her fussy baby, "nursing won't help; put some rum on her gums to settle the pain."

This class was part of Mission Robinson, a broad nationwide education outreach effort in Venezuela. Against this brief description of a literacy class, consider Margaret Atwood's poem "A Poor Woman Learns to Write," which centers on an illiterate peasant working laboriously to print her name with a stick in the dirt. The woman never thought that she could do it, the poet notes, not her—this lofty writing business was for much more important people than her. But she does do it; she prints her name, "her first word so far"; and she looks up and smiles.

The woman in the poem—like the students in Mission Robinson—is living out a universal rhythm that embodies education at its very best: she simply wrote her name, but in the process she changed herself forever, and she altered, then, the conditions of her life. As the adults in Mission Robinson write their words, they also transform their circumstances—in small ways, perhaps, but who can know where it will lead?—and another world becomes, suddenly and surprisingly, possible. This is the magic that awaits us in every classroom.

BUILDING THE ENVIRONMENT FOR LEARNING

**Key concept
A classroom is any space with or without walls where people assemble with an expectation of teaching and learning.**

Imagine your first (or your next) **classroom**. Open the door and peek in. Look around; take that first tentative step forward. This classroom is yours! You're neither a visitor nor a tourist nor a casual acquaintance any longer. This will soon become home base for you and for a yet unseen group of young people, and it's now tied up with your dynamic and developing teacher identity. Take another step, a bolder one this time. And another.

You're a teacher now, and this space will be a public reflection of you: your preferences and priorities and expectations for your students and for yourself, your sense of what knowledge and learning are all about, your choices, your standards and experiences—all of this and more is worked up and embodied in your learning environment. Right from the start it's essential to think as deeply as you can about all of it: What knowledge and experiences are of most value? What core beliefs about people, about human dignity and freedom, about democracy, about learning and living a good life will be apparent for all to see and experience?

Now is the best time to take stock, perhaps to make a list of core values that will become a part of your classroom no matter what. Write it up, write it down. Post it on your wall or your bathroom mirror. Carry it around in your pocket. Call it "MY CLASSROOM COMMITMENTS: *No Matter What!*"

Take the elegant but straightforward idea that *every human being is a three-dimensional creature much like yourself; a person with hopes, dreams, skills, and experiences; each with a body, a mind, and a spirit that must somehow be valued, respected, and represented in your classroom and somehow taken into account in your teaching.* If you take this as a value you intend to carry in your pocket into the classroom—if it's something you want to take as an ironclad commitment to live out every day *no matter what*—and to embed deep within the classroom structure, culture, and environment, it challenges you to find concrete ways to reject and resist actions that treat students as objects and any gestures that erase, obliterate, ignore, or silence any other human being. This is easy enough to say, this simple injunction, but excruciatingly difficult to enact in the daily lives of schools or classrooms, especially in places where labeling students, sorting them into hierarchies, and managing their behaviors have become the commonplace markers of good teaching. How will you deal with this? What alternative markers will represent and illuminate your valuing of students' lives?

Focus point

Make a list of core values that will become a part of your classroom no matter what.

Next to this core value, then, you might begin to make a second list, the beginnings of a chart—perhaps "Ten Action Steps Toward Realizing My Dream." So say you agree, and you have this first value listed: respect for persons, full recognition of the humanity of everyone who enters my classroom. How will that look concretely in practice? What demands does it make? What will you do (and promise yourself never to do) in your teaching? You will need to generate some ideas, some actual items that could bring this value to life in the trembling and messy reality of a gaggle of real kids in real school time and real school space. Maybe your chart is morphing into a system of file folders bristling with practical arts, curricular projects, instructional approaches, possible trips into the community, readings, free writes, books, story starters, guest speakers, aesthetic considerations, visitors, poetry, music and songs, work assignments, websites, films, community resources, recipes, community service possibilities, physical challenges, and encounters with the arts. One folder might be titled "The Physical Environment"; it would denote places for each student to keep his or her work and materials, spaces for students to express and create, both individually and together, and perhaps a wall dedicated to "our families and our community." A folder marked "Routine and Rhythm of the Day" might include ideas for an opening class meeting geared toward building a culture of respect and recognition, and for a closing activity to note the accomplishments of the day and to anticipate tomorrow. "Management Issues" might include reminders (Note to self: Never threaten or humiliate a kid, no matter what!) and positive plans (I'll have only a single rule posted, and work out all problems in this light: "This is our learning environment, and we treat one another and one another's work with generous respect").

Now take another step into your classroom. You're a unique human being, a person unlike any other, and this space ought to reflect that singular humanity. You're also now a teacher, and this classroom is one place where your teaching will be enacted and your full humanity lived. As you build your classroom, remember your commitments and your expectations for both yourself and your students. How do you want to live here with twenty-five or thirty other people? What are you inviting them into?

Some classrooms embody reading and writing, and they announce in a zillion ways that literacy in all its forms is valued here. This is likely something you'll want to establish from the start: books, magazines, comics everywhere; an author's corner and a cozy space to curl up with reading materials; the walls bristling with student writing, drafts, and edits; an author of the week featured at one table. Other classrooms give other messages: sit down and be quiet; face front because all knowledge is at the front; be obedient and compliant. What messages will your space embody and communicate? Go back and keep adding to your "*No Matter What!*" list.

You have to start to figure out how you're going to live here with some degree of satisfaction, comfort, ease, and even joy, and that won't happen unless you take initiative to breathe life into the environment from the start. Look at it. Walk around in it. Smell and touch it. Now ask yourself how you're going to make this space your own. A house is not a home, as the old song says; it needs people and love to bring it to life. A classroom is not a learning environment, either, at least not automatically. Not yet. Get busy.

Right away you might want to bring in some plants and pets, or your favorite music and magazines, or paintings or posters or poems, or chess and backgammon and Go, or perhaps a small fridge and a coffeemaker. Books, for sure—books and books and books. You don't want to check your personhood at the door, or to pretend that you're just an interchangeable cog in a mass impersonal machine called school. Whatever makes some spot your own place, however you write your signature on a space, do it here and do it now. The point is to set down some of your unique human roots. Put those things on your list too.

The classroom will reflect your humanity, but because
the classroom belongs to the students as well, it will reflect or diminish the humanity of each of them, too—
maybe they should bring in pets and plants and poems
and books, just as you're planning to do. The trick is to
be bold and modest, assertive but humble. The received
wisdom of teaching tells you to keep everything neat and
systematized, chairs in a row, teacher front and center,
behavioral charts in view, the engineering of learning
embodied in the room arrangement, but is this how *you*
see learning and growth? What does each of your students need? And just as important, what does each one
bring? What do you need, and what do you bring? What
are the consequences of your teaching for these students?

This is one of the great challenges of teaching: you will
find that every student you encounter is an unruly spark
of meaning-making energy on a voyage of discovery and
surprise; that is, you will learn that each is unique, like
you, each a dynamic work in progress, unfinished, contingent, leaning forward. If you decide to embrace that
diversity (as opposed to spending gobs and stacks of energy denying and suppressing it), your classroom will of
necessity become a work in progress as well, unfinished,
ever changing, and contingent. Put it on your list. You
can't build a generic classroom, a place for all people and
all times, and then keep it clean and orderly and hum-
ming along over the next thirty years. Each year is different, each child presents new opportunities and different
challenges, and each group has its own dynamics and per-
sonalities. You need to make the classroom your own, for
sure, and simultaneously you need to give the classroom
away. This is never an easy thing to do.

Of course, this classroom isn't your *only* place on
earth—you don't live behind the chalkboard or under-
neath the desk; you have a home, a community, a family,
and a bunch of social groups you call your own—and it
isn't yours alone. *This classroom will belong as well to every
student who walks through the door and, through each of*

Focus point

them, to every family and friend, every network and connection, every concentric circle of community. Take a deep breath. This expansive, collective sense of ownership, participation, and presence—this feeling that a trillion threads of humanity are happily haunting the place—is really exciting, but it can get super complicated too. A big challenge for you will be to help each one find a way to claim it, to resource and redefine it, to vitalize those ghosts, and finally to own it. You'll be figuring this out for a long, long time, so file it away. There's a whole lot of history and humanity worked up in here already, and a lot more to come, so let's go back to the beginning: this classroom is yours.

Every built environment reflects a range of ideas, values, preferences, instincts, and experiences. You need to think now about how your deepest moral commitments toward people, youth, and teaching will be made manifest and become embodied in your classroom—about how you will create a space that's an extension of those values. Imagine that

Focus point

a year from now some of us will drop by your classroom to see how you're doing: What do you hope that we would immediately realize about you and your teaching intentions simply by walking through the door? What artifacts of learning and teaching would be readily apparent, and what would we surely find by digging a little deeper?

It's up to you to decide how to build an environment that purposefully and intentionally displays what you value for yourself and for your students. Will it challenge and nurture the wide range of people who will actually pass through your classroom door? Will it be a space where students are visible and expected to use their minds well, to derive knowledge from information, to invest thought with courage, to connect consciousness to conduct, to tell their own stories, ask their own questions, and pursue their own answers? Put those items on your list, and make connecting arrows to all the practical things you plan to do to make them real.

Build an environment that purposefully and intentionally displays what you value for yourself and for your students.

Schools can be places where the artificial division of the world into subjects, the huge numbers of students, and the rational organization and scheduling of everything from bodily functions to creative expression are the norm. In these places, people often have difficulty being authentic. Whether compliant or resistant, sweet or surly, students are not always available, accessible, or visible to themselves or others in school. How will you encourage and support your students? Add those methods to the list.

ATMOSPHERE, EXPERIENCE, TECHNIQUE, VOICE

The teacher builds the context, and the dimensions you work with are not just feet and inches but also hopes and dreams. There must be multiple entry points toward learning and a range of routes to success if you hope to teach every student. They're all different, and if your commitment is to teach them all, you cannot escape that responsibility by passing some and flunking others. Think about what one senses when walking through the door: What is the atmosphere? What quality of experience is anticipated? What technique is dominant? What voice will be apparent?

Is the *atmosphere* like a workshop for doing things or a trade show demonstrating dazzling and efficient stuff? Is it a quiet place to look but not touch, or a formal garden for meditation? Is it an information desk, a video arcade, a laboratory, an exposition hall, an author's or a dancer's studio, a gallery, a retreat, a stage, or a control room? Is it some combination?

Would the *experience* be group problem-solving and planning, sharing or individual? Does it break through walls and spill into the world? Is there room for public play, private reflection, or some mixture? Is it browsing, finding your way, getting wet, having fun? Is there a

The teacher builds the context, and the dimensions you work with are not just feet and inches but also hopes and dreams.

chance for pretend and make-believe, fabrication and invention, speculation and rehearsal, or imitation?

Will there be *techniques* that emphasize sensory immersion, hands-on work, group games, or careful and sustained observation? Will students be at the controls? How will that happen? Will invention and imagination be invited into the room? Will your classroom involve scale shifts, such as building a huge heart to walk through like the one in the museum? Why? Why not?

Will the teacher's *voice* be authoritative, impersonal, dramatic, informative, welcoming, comic, awesome, silly, earnest, purposeful, or each in turn? Will the teacher's voice invite other voices into the conversation?

All of these questions are in the service of trying to build an environment that serves your largest and deepest purposes. The answers all belong on the list: *no matter what!*

Teaching involves the courage and the imagination to give your energy and your time and *yourself* to others. It involves learning to talk with the hope of being heard, and, perhaps more important, it involves listening with the possibility of being changed. In the noise and confusion of the modern world and of today's classrooms, listening can be an act of empathy and resistance, a gesture of recognition, an act of love. Teaching assumes that every human being can go beyond, that we can indeed make the world a better place. There is a hopefulness built into the enterprise: there may be defeat after defeat after defeat, there may be setbacks and tears, but we get up and we try again. Teaching is the craft of rebuilding, redefining, and respiriting, again and again.

Teaching is the craft of rebuilding, redefining, and respiriting, again and again.

CREATING A DEMOCRATIC CULTURE

All schools in all places and all times serve the societies in which they're embedded—authoritarian schools serve authoritarian systems, apartheid schools serve apartheid society, and so on. School people everywhere want their students to study hard, learn the curriculum, stay away from harmful drugs and alcohol, complete their homework, and so on. In fact, none of these features distinguishes schools in the old Soviet Union or fascist Germany or medieval Saudi Arabia or apartheid South Africa from schools in a democracy, and indeed many of those other school systems produced great artists and athletes, scientists, and generals. Surely many teachers in those other societies worked hard, struggled with management and discipline issues, and brought energy, commitment, and concern for the young with them into their classrooms. But those systems lacked an essentially democratic culture, and so they also produced obedience and conformity, moral blindness and easy agreement, obtuse patriotic nationalism and a willingness to follow orders right into the furnaces. And most—certainly not all—teachers went along.

In a democracy, one would expect something radically different and something more—a commitment to free inquiry, questioning, and participation; a push for access and equity; a curriculum that encouraged independent thought and singular judgment; a standard of full recognition of the humanity of each individual.

Schools for obedience and conformity are characterized by authoritarianism and irrelevance, passivity and fatalism. They turn on the little technologies for control and normalization; twisted schemes for managing the crowd; knotted systems of rules and discipline; exhaustive machinery of schedules and clocks; laborious and often irrelevant programs of testing and grading; assessment, judgment, and evaluation whose purpose is merely to create an elaborate chart that sorts winners from losers, all of it adding up to an intricately constructed hierarchy—everyone in a designated place, and a place for everyone. Knowing and accepting one's pigeonhole on the vast and barren mountainside becomes the core of teaching, and the only lesson one is apparently expected to need. And, of course, none of this is worthy of the soul of democracy, none of it an expression of a living and breathing democratic culture.

The African American thinker and educator Carter G. Woodson wrote his great work *The Mis-Education of the Negro* in 1933, with the central argument turning on these issues. He warned us of the power that schools have to make people stupid:

> When you control a man's thinking you do not have to worry about his actions. You do not have to tell him not to stand here or go yonder. He will find his "proper place" and will stay in it. You do not need to send him to the back door. He will go without being told. In fact, if there is no back door, he will cut one for his special benefit. His education makes it necessary.

"His education makes it necessary"—the stakes for Woodson were both stupendous and monstrous: participatory democracy versus an empty shell, a nation of sheep versus a collective of free human beings, liberation versus slavery.

The core lessons of a democratic education—an education for citizenship, participation, and active engagement—include the belief that each human being is unique and induplicable and of incalculable value; that everyone has a mind of his or her own to nourish and develop; that we are each a work in progress swimming through a dynamic history in the making toward an uncertain and indeterminate shore; that we can choose to join with others and act on our own judgments and our own imaginations; and that human enlightenment and liberation are always the result of thoughtful choice and action.

There is a far greater purpose and a much more fundamental goal driving teaching in a democracy than either loyalty to the state or fealty to the leaders or job training: we are geared toward empowering free people to think

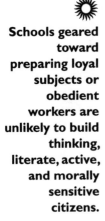

Schools geared toward preparing loyal subjects or obedient workers are unlikely to build thinking, literate, active, and morally sensitive citizens.

freely about all the issues that affect their lives, to imagine wild and colorful alternatives, and then to step up boldly toward their dreams. Pressure from the state to make schools little outposts of patriotic nationalism or military recruitment, or from businesses to make education exclusively serve corporate needs, jeopardizes the democratic foundations of education. Schools geared toward preparing loyal subjects or obedient workers are unlikely to build thinking, literate, active, and morally sensitive citizens who carry out their democratic responsibilities to one another, to their communities, and to the earth.

Participatory democracy rejects exclusively formal and structural markers of self-governance in favor of people actually making the decisions that affect their lives. Voting is surely important, for example, but it is not, in and of itself, a singular or sturdy marker of democracy. Nazi Germany, the Soviet Union, and Baathist Iraq all held elections, but none was a recognizably democratic society because each lacked the spirit and the culture of democracy. In our own country, we've seen elections stolen and manipulated, voters disenfranchised and their rights suppressed, and electoral colleges or the Supreme Court overturning a popular vote. Elections may be an essential right and a necessary aspect of democracy, but they are also by themselves an insufficient expression.

What does it mean concretely and distinctly, then, to be an excellent teacher in and for a democratic society? What makes a democratic classroom unmistakable? To begin, it is a place where we strive consciously to learn and practice a commitment to, and the values of, self-governance: to care for other people; to accept wild and vast diversity as the norm; to acknowledge that the full development of each is the condition for the full development of all; and to honor and welcome participation, free thought and speech, civil liberties, human rights, and social equality. Curriculum that contributes to these commitments involves analysis and exploration, different thinking and divergent political expression, independent thought and a wide range of action, and access to an intellectually rich experience. Good items for your list, yes?

In a democracy we want our students to be able to think for themselves and to make judgments based on evidence and argument. We want them to learn to ask essential questions that are—like the students themselves—always in motion, dynamic, and never twice the same: Who in the world am I? How did I get here and where am I going? What in the world are my choices and my chances? What's my story, and how is it like or unlike the stories of others— my family, my community, people who are nearby and others who are far, far away? What is my responsibility to each and to all of them? In many ways these kinds of questions are themselves the answers, the very frame of a democratic teaching agenda; and part of our job, then, becomes keeping these questions vital, alive, and fresh in our classrooms as we search for ways to live within and beyond whatever contingent and partial answers we and our students might discover along the way.

Participatory democracy insists that the people themselves get active in the public square. Mass society is an obstacle; the manipulation of media a barrier; huge amounts of money a hindrance; bureaucracy, hierarchy, command-style organization an obstruction. So is the pressure of the uniculture, the power of the monologue, the symbol of the spin doctor and the talking head. All of this can itself become grist for the classroom mill— objects of curiosity, investigation, and interrogation within the classroom and the curriculum.

Teachers and students can challenge orthodoxy, dogma, and mindless complacency; be skeptical of all authoritative claims; interrogate and trouble the given and the taken-for-granted. The growth of knowledge, insight, and understanding depends on that kind of effort, and the inevitable clash of ideas that follows must be nourished and not crushed. It's all part of living in a democratic culture. Teachers have a fundamental responsibility to organize classrooms as sites of open discussion, free of coercion or intimidation. Students should recognize that a classroom can only be relatively safe, that arguing about ideas cannot be risk-free. Feeling uncomfortable about one's beliefs—students and teachers alike—is a matter of course in good classrooms.

Democratic pedagogy, as W. E. B. Du Bois noted, is geared not so much to making men into carpenters but to insisting that carpenters can become men, by which he meant full, diverse, and three-dimensional human beings, naming their own predicaments, asking questions of the universe, and constructing their own lives. To alienate people from their own judgments is to turn them into objects. To prevent people from naming their situations, entanglements, and predicaments is a form of violence.

Classrooms for democracy require problem-posing, question-asking, and dialogue—each one speaking with the hope of being heard, and each one listening with the possibility of being changed. If we want our students to be free and active in the range of democratic possibilities, we need to ask ourselves, are we showing them—through the examples of our own lives—how it's done? Put that at the top of your list.

EMBRACING CONTRADICTIONS

If I move to the neighborhood where I teach, am I a gentrifier or a community member? If I work in a charter school, am I abandoning the public space? Can I work for social justice and embrace the capitalist system? How should I think of myself, and how should I locate my teaching in the big picture? There are no easy answers, and we must make our wobbly ways into teaching as best we can, with ambiguity, uncertainty, incompleteness, and flawed reality our constant companions.

There are other even deeper contradictions at the heart of democracy and education that we acknowledge right from the start: if every human being is to be fully recognized and respected, each taken to be of incalculable value, if each is assumed to be walking a singular path across the earth, each with a distinct mark to be made, then each student is somehow sacred. And an acceptance of sacredness demands that we embrace the full humanity of every student—that we validate them as persons as we search for and find ways to take their side. But as we work extra hard to become sensitive to how they see themselves, who they are, and who they are becoming, we find ourselves in conflict with all the forces mobilized in schools to standardize and sum up, to sort and label, to aggregate and regulate.

There is an often-precarious balance between individual and group needs.

The conflict lies between the democratic goal—and frankly, the teacher goal—that directs itself to the full development of the human personality and to the strengthening of mutual respect for human rights and fundamental freedoms, and the capitalist goals of relentless production and ever-expanding consumption as unquestioned "goods" in themselves. Fighting to hold on to and find ways to enact our best thinking about learning and teaching, our commitment to democracy, and our deepest values about students in the sometimes harsh world of real schools is often arduous. Teachers in the purest capitalist tradition develop hierarchies of producers and consumers, of workers and managers as they work to maximize efficiency, production, and the rationalized use of human resources; teachers in a participatory democracy work to resist the overspecialization of human activity—the separation of the intellectual from the manual, the head from the hand, or the heart from the head, the creative and the functional—as a distortion, and build instead on the unity of human beings, a unity based on recognition of differences as well as consciousness of interdependence. The two prototypes are in conflict, interacting uneasily at best.

There is an often-precarious balance between individual and group needs. Democracy honors and values each person; simultaneously, democracy honors and values the community. This is a conflict that erupts in every classroom from kindergarten through graduate school: circle time versus free play, group discussion or personal projects, collective problem-solving as opposed to individual expression. Classrooms are sites of learning to live together, of individual growth and social responsibility, entrepreneurial impulse and socialist spirit, side by side in practice.

Acknowledging these tensions is a step toward addressing them, but addressing them does not mean settling them easily. In fact, teachers who put the tensions too lightly to rest by embracing one or the other branch will find themselves less productive with students and ultimately dissatisfied with themselves. The alternative is to choose contradiction as a space within which to live and to struggle, a place to teach.

To say either "My job is to get kids ready for the real world, for society as it is" or "My job is to water the little seedlings and watch them grow" is to misunderstand the contradiction and reduce the complexity. The real world? Which one? Some might argue that the real world is vicious, tough, unfair, competitive, warlike, and mean. Should we turn our preschools, then, into little drill squadrons for three-year-olds, our high schools into boot camps for teenagers?

And on the other side, the watering-the-seeds side: lots of teachers who want desperately to be kind and to be liked can also fail to challenge kids to read. "I love these kids so much," one might say, "and their lives are so hard, I just want to nurture them." If you "love" your students but fail to show them the ways the world works, the ways power, for example, is hidden and horded, disguised and denied, or the ways injustice is made to seem inevitable—if you fail in this, you have really failed to teach them well, and that is not exactly an act of love; failing to teach them to read is not an act of love. So the tension: teach them to read as an act of love; struggle to nourish and challenge in the same gesture; respect the people who walk through the door, embrace them as fellow human beings, and invite and push them toward deeper and wider ways of knowing, toward that wider world they will inherit and are destined to change.

FINDING THE WISDOM IN THE ROOM

But first things first: you must work hard to become the best teacher you possibly can be. To teach is to choose a life of challenge. A first and fundamental challenge is to see your students—beyond the blizzard of labels based on deficits—as three-dimensional creatures, people of heart, mind, and spirit *just like yourself*. This can be excruciatingly difficult to bring to life in environments infected with the toxic habit of labeling or seized by the deadening obsession of standardized ways of seeing and knowing. Against that hard reality you must seek the wisdom in the room.

Every student is an expert on his or her own life. If a child is hurt or angry, thrilled or overjoyed, bored or distracted, recognition of those feelings is supporting the child's integrity. Conscientious teachers ask themselves all the time what it is that they need to know in order to be successful with this kid, or with this one, or this one. Surely knowledge of subject matter and the curriculum and the disciplines is an important part of the answer. As is, of course, knowledge about the school and its expectations. And don't forget knowledge of yourself. But central to everything else is knowledge about the student, the child or the young person before you.

Looking at our students draws us deeper into the contexts and circumstances of their lives—family, community, culture, and on and on—and we seek, then, greater knowledge of the society and the world we're initiating youngsters into. This is not only vast but also dynamic, so our work is definitely cut out for us. The unexamined teaching life is hardly worth living, but the examined life

is full of pain and difficulty—the contexts of our lives include unearned privileges and undeserved suffering,
murderous drugs and crushing work, a howling sense of
hopelessness for some, and the palpable threat of annihi-
lation for others. To be aware of the social and moral
universe we inhabit and share—aware, too, of what has
yet to be achieved in terms of human possibility—is to
be a teacher capable of hope and struggle, of outrage and
joy and action.

We approach the moral heart of teaching as it is lived
in the crucible of a classroom. Here we focus on teaching
as intellectual and ethical work, something beyond the
instrumental and the linear. *Teaching requires thoughtful,
caring people to carry it forward successfully, and we need,
then, to commit ourselves to becoming more caring and
more thoughtful as we grow steadily into our work.*

Focus point

If we teachers hope to contribute to rescuing teaching
from the tangle of its discontents, we must get smart
about the real dimensions of democracy, and we must
rearticulate and reignite—and try to live out in our daily
classroom lives—the basic proposition that in a democracy, life is geared toward and powered by the radical notion that the fullest development of all human beings is
the necessary condition for the full development of each
person, and, conversely, that the fullest development of
each is necessary for the full development of all. We assume, and set out to find, the wisdom in the room.

It's obvious in classroom life that the unity of human
beings is based on recognition of our multiple differences. People are different, and we are all interdepen-
dent. What we can live out in a classroom is a kind of
social generosity, a knowledge based on recognition of
our unity, our solidarity. We can note that knowledge is
inherently a public good, that it can be reproduced at
practically no cost, and that, unlike many other things,
when you give knowledge away you don't have any less
of it. In a sensible society, and surely in our classrooms,
knowledge is shared widely and without restriction.

CONCLUSION

To be a good teacher in and toward democracy means to have faith in people and to believe in the possibility that people can create and change things. *The classroom, then, is not preparation for life so much as it is life itself, an active process in which everyone—students and teachers—participates together.*

Focus point

The fundamental message of the teacher, after all, is this: you can change your life. Whoever you are, wherever you've been, whatever you've done, the teacher invites you to a second chance, another round, perhaps a different conclusion. As students and teachers begin to see themselves as linked to one another, as tied to history and capable of collective action, the fundamental message of teaching becomes broader, more generous: we must change ourselves as we come together to change the world. Teaching invites transformations; it urges revolutions small and large. The teacher posits possibility, openness, and alternative; the teacher points to what could be, but is not yet. The teacher beckons you to change your path, and so she has but one basic rule, which is to reach.

But of course the teacher can only create a context, set a stage, open a curtain. The teacher's task is excruciatingly complex precisely because it is idiosyncratic and improvisational—as inexact as a person's mind or a human heart, as unique and inventive as a friendship or a love affair. The teacher's work embraces background, environment, setting, surround, position, situation, connection. And relationship. Teaching is tougher than learning in this essential respect: teaching requires the teacher to *let learn*. Learning requires action, choice, and assent from the student. Teaching, then, is undertaken with hope, but without guarantees. Teaching is an act of faith.

The great Chilean poet Pablo Neruda wrote a poem to his fellow writers called "The Poet's Obligation," in which he instructed them in their core responsibility: You must, he said, become aware of your sisters and brothers who are trapped in subjugation and meaninglessness, imprisoned in ignorance and despair. You must move in and out of windows carrying a vision of the vast oceans just beyond the bars of the prison—a message of hope and possibility. Neruda ends with this: it is through me that freedom and the sea will call in answer to the shrouded heart. This could be the credo for conscious and effective classroom teachers: your classroom can still become an oasis of freedom and a beacon for a better world. Make it happen in this corner of this space, right here, right now.

DISCUSSION QUESTIONS

1. What qualities or dispositions do you hope students will take from your classroom into the rest of their lives?

2. Can you describe how you will build an environment in which those qualities can be seen, modeled, practiced, understood, debated, and nourished?

3. What are three things you can do to be sure that every student is visible and fully present as a learner in your classroom?

FURTHER READING

Canada, Geoffrey. 1996. *Fist Stick Knife Gun: A Personal History of Violence in America*. New York: Beacon Press.
A memoir about growing up in the whirlpool of American violence.

Finnegan, William. 1999. *Cold New World: Growing Up in a Harder Country*. New York: Modern Library.
A narrative about being young in modern America.

Hoffman, Marvin. 2007. *"You Won't Remember Me": The Schoolboys of Barbiana Speak to Today*. New York: Teachers College Press.
An Italian priest works a miracle with marginalized youth.

Meier, Deborah. 2002. *The Power of Their Ideas: Lessons for America from a Small School in Harlem*. New York: Beacon Press.
A school reformer describes the essence of successful urban school change.

Rodriguez, Luis. *Always Running: Gang Days in L.A.* London: Marion Boyars Publishers.
An autobiography.
Wright, Richard. 1945/2008. *Black Boy.* New York: Harper.
An autobiography of coming of age young, gifted, black, and poor.

CHAPTER TWO

SLOW, ACTIVE, AND SURPRISING

Remaking Teaching Through the Arts

S UMMERTIME STRETCHES like hot gum; on the bottom of a shoe, that's not a great quality, but in a classroom, for a teacher working to propel her students up and over the hurdles of graduation and promotion, elastic, widening time can be a gift. In one summer-suspended class, a group of girls, all there because they had failed one or more classes during the fall-to-spring high school year, are watching a DVD of Lucille Clifton reading her poems. As the tape starts, the girls are squirming and loud; the fact that they are inside and still in school while summer starts outside the building—starts, for all practical purposes, without them—means that nearly everyone is feeling prickly and deprived. A few of the young women sit with slumped chests collapsed down onto bellies, heads heavily settled onto arms crossed and resting on tabletops, eyelids firmly shut. Most are distractedly watching the monitor while they talk to their nearest, or even farthest, friends. Then Clifton's voice rings out, and she is smiling as she begins:

homage to my hips

these hips are big hips.
they need space to
move around in.
they don't fit into little
petty places. these hips
are free hips.

The poem builds and Clifton's voice swells, and then she closes with a head roll and a neck snap:

these hips are magic hips.
i have known them
to put a spell on a man and
spin him like a top!

The girls are listening now, and giggling. Like them, Lucille Clifton is brown-skinned and full-bodied. Like theirs, her hips are substantial, for sure. But the students are young, ripe, smooth-skinned, and hickey-necked, while Clifton, as she speaks this frankly sexy word picture, is white-haired, a woman who is more likely at a grandmother's distance from these students than a mother's. Clifton continues:

poem in praise of menstruation

if there is a river
more beautiful than this
bright as the blood
red edge of the moon if
there is a river
more faithful than this
returning each month
to the same delta . . .

Where just a moment before chairs swiveled and girls chuckled appreciatively about how their own big bottoms might spin some pleasure for a lover and for themselves, now the room erupted in a frenzy of distancing pronouncements.

"Ooo, nasty."

"She crazy!"

"That is *not* right. Why would she write something like that? That's not a poem. It's not . . . it's nothing people want to hear."

Clifton kept right on reading. She finished her praise song and a few minutes later offered an elegy to her last period: "Well, girl, goodbye . . ." and "*Wasn't she beautiful?*" Then, some "wishes for sons," which includes the lines

> i wish them cramps.
> i wish them a strange town
> and the last tampon.
> i wish them no 7/11.

Each girl was rapt. They all orbited Clifton now, and as she finished with "in the inner city / or / like we call it / home," the room was nearly quiet; a few girls talked softly to each other, a young mother pulled a picture of her baby son from her purse and sat appreciating it, a couple of more girls were moving their pens over paper, and one asked who—what poet—were they going to hear next?

TEXTBOX 2.1

To read the wonderful poems cited here in full, see *Good Woman* for "homage to my hips" and *Quilting: Poems 1987–1990* for "poem in praise of menstruation," "to my last period," and "wishes for sons." More of Lucille Clifton's poems, her biography, and audio recordings are available at the website of the Poetry Foundation (www.poetryfoundation.org), and videos of Clifton reading her work can be found on YouTube (www.youtube.com).

THE ARTS AND SOCIAL JUSTICE

We—all of humanity—are artists. The record is clear: for at least tens of thousands of years humans have crafted artful responses to our surroundings. Adornment, embellishment, representation, documentation, self-expression, persuasion, innovation; we have always, it seems, engaged in these ways with our milieus, enjoying, improving, and sharing what we see and know, and even what we don't. Art has been, and continues to be, defined variously: it is the name we give to our common drive to note and create rhythm, harmony, and balance; it is how we express our experience of the mysterious and difficult to understand; it is the shapes, sounds, and movements we use to expose feelings, preserve the ephemeral, and suggest solutions. And we have, it seems, long interpreted and debated the meaning and place of art in society: Plato and Aristotle described art as *mimesis*, or a representation (though not a complete copy) of nature; Aristotle outlined one of the earliest arguments for art as a means of civic education. During the European Middle Ages artists were educated within guilds, and the goal was transmission of skills and attainment of traditional mastery. Art has also been posited as a *public good* that could and should be made widely available through common schools; a *significant form* that moves its viewers aesthetically (Bell 1914); a means to *heightened experience*, through which multiple senses may be engaged and the ordinary can come to seem extraordinary; a form of *cultural history*, through which social values are expressed and shared; and a means of *political action*, or even "the artist's political manifesto" (Mortier 2009).

Art, with its great capacity, can substantively and powerfully enrich both teaching and learning.

Art, with its great capacity, can substantively and powerfully enrich both teaching and learning; it offers the means to reach more students in more ways. But the implications of prioritizing the arts in education, of teaching about and through the arts at every point, are even bigger and more important for teachers. In this chapter we propose that art inoculates against what threatens to ruin and deaden education. Another way of saying this is, as public education is to society, art is to public education. We believe public education is an unassailable social good, a space where—although it is always in the making, like democracy—we come together to explore, nurture, and pass along ideas, skills, and much more. Universal public education insists that we all have capacity and value; the very fact of it mitigates, albeit imperfectly, against systemic social inequities. In a similar way, art, which is unruly, ambiguous, inherently nonstandard, and often subversive, wards off the problems linked to institutionalization—sameness, dullness, rote-not-vital relations and activities. We hope here to counter the common sense of art in education—that it is an add-on, an "extra" that can be included or not in school, that it is not fundamentally important to the prospect of becoming educated and, in fact, a crucial way of knowing and engaging the world—with an exploration of art as integral to the project of teaching for justice.

The philosopher Hannah Arendt wrote that "education is the point at which we decide whether we love the world enough to assume responsibility for it and by the same token save it from that ruin which, except for renewal, except for the coming of the new and young, would be inevitable" (Arendt 1968, 196). This is a big charge, but art can support such an engaged, committed kind of teaching. For example, the teacher who observed her students and then organized a summer curriculum aimed at addressing their pressing concerns as well as their academic difficulties *acted* her love for the world when she introduced them to Lucille Clifton and invited them to write poetry of their own. Her teaching assumed big, good possibilities for her students—that the girls could learn to tell their stories as powerfully as Clifton and that, when artfully represented, these views and experiences would enrich us all.

**Key concept
Social justice
refers to a focus
on human rights
and social equity.**

Like *all* good teaching, this teaching engaged **social justice** themes and practices. For example, it stimulated *self-awareness*, centering reflection on the question of "What is important to you?" It fostered *democracy* by proposing that everyone can participate and every story can be valued. It supported *collectivity*, or a sense that we are all in it together and that our experiences are shared. And it stemmed from other related premises, including *activism*, or choosing and acting; *public space*, or bringing world to classroom and classroom to world; *history*, as in, we are always making it, even in the midst of the seemingly mundane; and, perhaps most important for justice-focused work, *imagination* that exceeds limitation or, as the poet Jayne Cortez described it, dreaming up "somewhere in advance of nowhere" (quoted in Kelley 2002, xii).

Of course, this isn't an exhaustive list and there isn't a manual for social justice work, either in or out of schools. As Myles Horton, the popular educator and co-founder with poet Don West of Tennessee's Highlander Folk School, wrote in his autobiography, *The Long Haul:*

> When I speak about a social goal, the goal for society, and for myself, I don't say, "This is exactly what it's going to be like." I don't have a blueprint in mind. I'm thinking more of a vision, I'm thinking of direction. I'm thinking of steps. I'm thinking more in terms of signs pointing in the right direction than I am of the shape of future society, because I don't know what that shape is going to be. (1990, 226)

Horton noted that when linked to personal urgencies and the possibility of social change—learning to read to be able to register to vote, for example—skills acquire powerful meaning. This insight shaped the work of Highlander's Citizenship Schools, which taught literacy as just "one step toward . . . becoming citizens and social activists" (Horton 1990, 100) during the civil rights movement. Horton knew that education is always more than a tactic or strategy, no matter how tactical or strategic; he wasn't just educating voters, he was aiming to change the world. Even without a map, we can each lean into that future, as teachers and through our work in schools—it's not orthodoxy (right thinking), but ortho*praxy* (right doing) that will move us there, action by action, poem by poem.

TEXTBOX 2.2

Highlander Folk School, now called the Highlander Research and Education Center (www.highlandercenter.org), has always emphasized the importance of the arts to social justice and offered classes in music and visual arts. Among the many activists who have taught, learned, and played at Highlander are Virginia Durr, Martin Luther King Jr., Rosa Parks, and Pete Seeger.

THE EXPANSIVE POSSIBILITIES OF IMAGINATION

Too often teaching is discussed as if its primary concerns were technical, mere matters of arranging time and furniture well, or of plotting the flow of tasks in this or that way, or focusing narrowly enough that tests can catch the outcome. This push is not good for teachers, who must have room to wander, diverge, and invent in their work, which is, when done the way it should be done, profoundly creative. It is not good for students either, for exactly the same reason. And here is where art enters.

Art in all its forms, from poetry and performance to painting, sculpture, and music, and newer varieties including site-based, digital, and public practices, offers opportunities for teachers and students to counter the commonsense constraints of schooling. Assessment is one example; all students tasked with art projects can make the case that

Focus point

Teachers must have room to wander, diverge, and invent in their work.

there is no really good way to grade what they produce, and most art teachers would agree—art isn't about getting right answers, or even making things that require effort, are well crafted, and look or sound beautiful (although teachers often focus on these qualities when assessing student work). Rather, poems, performances, and paintings are investigations and processes—the journey is what is most important, not the unknown end. That is why art is the perfect form for schools and teachers, particularly for those who are interested in social justice goals and values; it is all about taking one step after another, *for* the steps and not just the destinations. And it offers this opportunity to move down a path, discovering together as the outcome of interplay among teachers, students, and the art.

Return to the poetry, and the girls listening, and the teacher hovering just out of view; this scene unfolded first as a plan, then as a simmering surprise. The original curriculum had to give way to the girls' unknowns: What would they make of all this body talk? Could they take the blood? Would Clifton's words ring true? How many poems should or, perhaps more to the point, *would* they listen to? The teacher could plan, but not predict. Art opens up over time, through repetition of forms and themes; the girls needed time, too, to take the words in, to open up, and to finally connect. Art offers some perspectives that can be used as tools by teachers; in fact, this chapter proposes that some specific art-generated tools can be used as a framework for every part of education. The first and most important of these is: *take it slow.*

Slow teaching. The language is inspired by a movement with myriad emerging aspects or flows—slow food, slow journalism, slow travel, slow listening, and, yes, slow education.

Each of these versions of slow living insists that we all take many, many deep breaths and let experience expand out in the most leisurely, sensuous ways possible. A call

TEXTBOX 2.3

Read manifestos, platforms, and inspirational statements for all these varieties of slow engagement at their many websites. For slow food, see www.slowfood.com and www.slowfoodusa.org. *Slow journalism* was coined by journalist Naka Nathaniel; video of a 2008 discussion about the concept can be seen at http://annenberg.usc .edu/CentersandPrograms/ProfessionalEducation/GettyArtsJourn/ SlowJour.aspx. A manifesto for slow travel is available at www.slow traveleurope.eu/slow-travel-manifesto. Slow listening is explored at slowlisteningmovement.blogspot.com. And a discussion of slow education is online at www.slowmovement.com/slow_schools.php.

to slow education points to the fact that even in our hurry-up, instant-everything world, the growth of a child takes time. Slow living in its variety invites dawdlers and roamers; it encourages veering and diving deep. Specifically, it calls for attention to, and appreciation of, the local; the development of sustainable systems; and slow, slow, pleasurable engagements. This kind of *slow* can be a guide for art in general, but particularly in schools, where the context of children's lives (the local), the classroom and building community (the sustainable), and the projects undertaken (the slow and pleasurable) are the qualities of powerful teaching, whatever the subject. In fact, teachers can push back at the restricting structures of schooling by incorporating art into everything they do and pointing out to all concerned that good teaching and good art both take time and room to wander.

Teachers can push back at the restricting structures of schooling by incorporating art into everything they do.

In recent writings, Richard Sennett (2008) and Malcolm Gladwell (2008) have made the point that excelling at anything, including art and craft—here defining both as William Morris (1883) did when he exclaimed, "Art is [every person's] expression of [his or her] joy in labor" (the original is written in capital letters and the androcentric

Artistry is a human birthright.

language of that time; for ease on the eyes and conscience we have altered both)—requires hours, days, and years of practice. Incremental development is the key—"slow but go," as a friend has encouraged.

This is important for teaching: art is not the sole province of those who call themselves *artists;* in fact, artistry is a human birthright. In this way, though, it is no different in kind from all knowledge—we humans learn; that is our common condition. This is a very different claim from assertions that some people have special inborn talent or genius. What time allows us is the opportunity to keep at it, to repeat and reflect, repeat and revise, repeat and appreciate, and repeat and reflect again. In fact, Gladwell (2008, 41) argues that every person considered a "prodigy" or exquisitely skilled has dedicated ten thousand hours or ten years of repetition to develop what may now look like effortless expertise. But he also notes that gaining that vast amount of practice is difficult; few will be able to do it alone, and most will need "some kind of extraordinary opportunity that gives them a chance to put in those hours" (Gladwell 2008, 42), which is where school and time can come together as *slow teaching*—a teacher's purposeful intervention in the clock-marked rush of each school day through the inclusion of art and the real time to participate through listening, touching, creating, reflecting, and beginning again and again.

Slow teaching, as a form of teaching for social justice, is "teaching against the grain" (Cochran-Smith 2004, 28); teachers committed to this kind of pedagogy can feel fearful and find themselves unsupported (Salas 2004). For this reason, and for the pleasure of it, educators should make it a priority to build connections with allies, including teachers in their own and other subject areas, administrators, students, parents, community members, and activists. Classrooms are not, should not, and cannot be islands; rather, they must be considered and created as hubs of inquiry and centers of action, with links to every important topic, movement, and social concern. Teachers aiming to develop a curriculum that bucks trends benefit from working in creative communication with the increasing number of progressive educator groups that can be found online, usually by Googling "teacher" and "social justice."

Although the girls listening to Clifton's poetry may not yet be writing their own lines—and Sennett and Gladwell are specifically addressing the act of creating— they *are* practicing what art always invites: imaginative sense-making. Russian psychologist Lev Vygotsky (1925/ 1971) viewed the arts as a stimulus to cognitive development and claimed that in the act of creating or viewing art, a "reply" is initiated—a transformation of the viewer's or creator's initial reaction to the work and of their understanding of limits. For example, a young student is presented with a photograph of her neighborhood and invited to design a new streetscape by filling in empty lots and vacant storefronts with anything she chooses. She begins a drawing that imagines her community with a carnival, a bakery with cupcake-filled windows, a colorfully painted school with an orchard "where kids can eat apples right from trees," a swimming pool and outdoor track, and an outdoor café with umbrellas where she can meet her friends. Her "act of envisioning opens up new possibilities . . . for further envisioning"; extending the project, her classmates hang their own drawings around the room, sparking excited discussion as the children admire and then expand on one another's city-planning ideas (Holloway and LeCompte 2001, 395). John Dewey wrote in *Democracy and Education* that "work which remains permeated with the play attitude is art" (quoted in Sennett 2008, 288); all teachers are art teachers when they invite their students to play with serious, albeit unpredictable, intent.

This capacity of art to trigger more and new thought makes it important for educators, of course, but its potential is even more expansive. The poet Gwendolyn

Brooks reminds us that art is "not an old shoe," soft and comfortable (quoted in Gayles 2003, 37). Often, she claims, "art hurts. Art urges voyages—and it is easier to stay at home." Vygotsky also described how the arts can "incite, excite, and irritate" (1925/1971, 252), stimulating in us the prospect of dreaming and acting in new ways, of pushing us to voyage in unknown places. Similarly, in her book *Releasing the Imagination*, philosopher Maxine Greene links the arts to the development of "social imagination: the capacity to invent visions of what should be and what might be in our deficient society, on the streets where we live, in our schools" (1995, 5). Like Brooks, she points out that rather than lulling or soothing, the arts "stimulate the 'wide-awakeness' so essential to critical awareness, most particularly when they involve a move to the imaginary" (quoted in Paley 1995, 7). Art, Greene suggests, can lead to social change because "to call for imaginative capacity is to work for the ability to see things as if they could be otherwise" (1995, 19). Once seen, new worlds and ways of being can be made. Another art-linked tool for teachers interested in the intersection of the arts and social justice, then, is: *allow action.*

A young teacher surges down the street with a group of sixth-grade boys and one hundred thousand other people; he and the boys are working hard to keep close to each other, a fraught task in the crowd that is swiftly and steadily marching for immigrant rights through the large midwestern city. Two of the boys are holding small video cameras, and the group occasionally stops so one of them can interview someone in the crowd. The others, like many at the massive march, are carrying hand-painted posters. In English and Spanish, these signs offer kid's-eye views of the march's many agendas.

"We are not illegal people, we are America."

"No more borders; no more discrimination."

"*No deportan a los inmigrantes.*"

One points out: "My parents work hard, they are not criminals."

Cross-Reference For a discussion of immigration and education, see Book 2, Chapter 1.

Each of these posters is carefully lettered, most using a bubble-letter font style reminiscent of the graffiti of hip-hop culture circa the 1980s, the time frame of the teacher's early youth (he is still *in* his later youth). The visual influence is no accident; hip-hop led him to activism and art, and those experiences and perspectives soon propelled him into teaching (although an early felony charge for tagging made getting certified more complicated than is usual).

Back in their classroom, the boys watch and log the footage and start the edits that will result in a short video. They have already invited the whole school community to attend a screening in the school cafeteria because many parents couldn't go to the march, either because they had to work or because they were afraid they might be arrested and deported. What started as a class discussion about his students' lives and concerns has grown into a multipart, many-week project. First, the students in each of the art classes turned their ideas into block prints while learning about the history of political prints and posters. This stage of the venture included a look at various lettering styles, some discussion of past and current social movements, image and text selection, and linoleum block carving and the printing of a set of proofs. Then they translated their small print images, using a gridding and transfer method, into large posters for the march. They documented and memorialized their participation in this event using digital video, and edited the film on their teacher's laptop computer. They also planned the after-school showing, making flyers for the school's halls and for students to take home as invitations. Throughout, the group explored urgent concepts, from stereotypes of immigrants to democratic access to and use of media.

Art educator David Robinson, in his book *SoHo Walls: Beyond Graffiti*, refers to the streets as "public galleries" (1990, 5). From this perspective, the project took place in many public galleries—classroom, streets, and auditorium—in a reminder that both art and learning can happen anywhere. Another view is that this teacher used every possibility and condition to move toward a more public education, an education drawing on and building the themes of social justice—his own history and skills, the students' worries, the event of the march, and their opportunity to reframe school as a learning community that includes families and school workers as well as teachers and students.

From both perspectives, context is everything: were it a different teacher or students, or another city or year, we would be telling you some other story. Maybe the one about the teacher who was inspired by the Hyperbolic Crochet Coral Reef, a project of the arts- and science-focused Institute for Figuring, to employ her elementary school art classes in researching and sewing a felt coral reef and all its inhabitants, which was then collaboratively assembled and installed in the school lunchroom. Or the one about the teacher who led a group of high school students angry about the imposition of school uniforms without their input to analyze the purposes of uniforms historically and then through the art of Andrea Zittel, who has designed her own daily-wear costumes (you can check these out at the smockshop within her Institute of Investigative Living at www.zittel.org), and J. Morgan Puett and Mark Dion, who worked with nurses to redesign their work clothes (see the exhibit *RN: The Past Present and Future of the Nurse's Uniform* at www.jmorganpuett.com/rn/index.html). After reviewing the task-specific clothing of everyone from kings and queens to firefighters and ballerinas, the students developed their own personally significant uniforms—along with a successful petition against mandatory uniforms at school (this wasn't actually part of the class project, but it was certainly inspired by it). And there are many other stories like these, about arts-based school projects that raise big questions—Who am I? What do I value? Why do I choose these, and not other, ways? How were the de-

cisions made and by whom? Where can I intervene?—
and teach real skills.

What holds across all these examples is the kind of
learning that can occur when an artfully engaged teacher
takes the time to learn about her students and situation,
and then seizes possibilities as they emerge. Everything is
opportunity; everything is grist for the goal of catalyzing
and sustaining the interest and participation of students.
This teaching is passion-driven (*I don't know how to sew
and I'm not sure where coral grows but, hey, I love this project and we'll learn together!*), flexible (*Wow, they are really
charged about that new policy; what can I do to connect to
their energy?*), and open to some ambiguity (*Will this
work? Will they "get" Zittel's work? Do I?*). It embraces this
maxim: *let it surprise.*

In a small city's last-choice high school, the one most
black, brown, and poor white students attend, a health
class begins. The room is stuffy, it's early in the morning,
and the teens are tired. The teacher speaks, and nobody
listens. A loudspeaker crackles out an announcement,
and nobody listens. The clock ticks. At last, the teacher
says loudly, "Today, class, we have a visitor." Students
shift slowly in their seats, yet few stop their muffled conversations. And then the visitor enters the room—a tow-
ering satin-and-velvet vulva, ruby, magenta, and violet, at
least seven feet top to bottom and four feet wide. It's
stunning, even shocking; students who were dozing a
moment ago are now alert. The teacher talks a bit more,
but still nobody is listening. Instead, all eyes are on the
giant vulva. Then the visitor begins to speak, or rather
the vulva does. She performs for the class; she paces the
front of the room, then moves down each tight aisle of
desks, making sure every student in the room has a
chance to get close to her satiny folds. The topic, she tells
the class, is sexual health.

"To have a healthy sexual life," the vulva says, "everyone needs to know some anatomy." As she speaks, she
gestures toward the large rosy-purple velvet clitoris over

her face, which is framed by shiny pink satin labia that flutter gently.

"For young women, it all starts here."

The students wrote their many questions down, and the vulva-performer answered what she could on the spot. The teacher listened carefully during the discussion and later read all the questions to assess the class's starting point—what did they know and where did the confusions lie?—and to ensure that all the topics would be addressed during the rest of the semester. And the lessons of the day unfolded slowly, as students continued to ponder their interaction with the artist in the vulva costume and what she said that day in class. What kind of work does she do during the rest of her time? Why would a person make and then wear a giant vulva? If this is art, what else is?

ART RESISTS STANDARDIZATION

Examples of the prompts, such as "Only one element of each kind" and "What would your best friend do?" can be found at http://en .wikipedia.org/ wiki/Oblique_ Strategies.

There are as many ways to participate in this kind of limit-loosening teaching as there are teachers and students, communities and schools, and here we suggest one starting point: bring some artists' inquiries to your project planning and problem-posing. You would do well to start with *Oblique Strategies* by Brian Eno and Peter Schmidt (2009). First published in 1975 and revised and reprinted many times since, it presents prompts, principles, and "dilemmas" (as Eno and Schmidt describe the strategies on their website, http://www.rtqe.net/Oblique Strategies/), created by artists to be fruitfully employed by anyone seeking ways to spark new thoughts and ways of working.

Eno and Schmidt, and arguably all artists, offer clues that can help us find new ways of considering what we might otherwise do as rote, new ways of seeing askance and askew; the gift of these for teachers is that "oblique strategies" can be applied to many kinds of undertakings. Similar to these are the gentle provocations offered by

Janfamily, a group of London-based artists who have documented their experiments in living in a book of photographs, *Janfamily: Plans for Other Days* (Janfamily 2005). These, like the assignments generated by artists Miranda July and Harrell Fletcher and posted at the website *Learning to Love You More—#33. Braid someone's hair, #52. Write the phone call you wish you could have*—invite us to consider why we see, eat, dress, and even sit and sleep as we do (July and Fletcher 2009). Anyone can do these assignments—and many have; past results are posted for all to see at the *Learning to . . .* website. Each of these could be expanded to focus on a specific skill or subject, building from the absorbing delight or puzzlement the art can trigger.

Furthermore, seeing these online indicates the ways art forms and practices are evolving with new technologies. Finally, each of these and many, many other online arts sites—from LTTR with its compendium of artist projects, including examples of one thousand specially designed knit gloves by fiber artist Liz Collins (look elsewhere online for her sock monkey clothing), and both sari-wrapping and dance lessons as examples of "non commodified exchange" (www.lttr.org); to Red 76, with its radio transmitter workshops and laundry lectures (www.red76.com); to the Green Museum, and its many artists working with sustainability and environmental themes (www.greenmuseum.org); to others easily found via your favorite search engine—offer a range of opportunities for teachers to engage all students in "outside the lines" ways of thinking and acting. This is always important and seems especially urgent now.

The shift from supporting fully public schools to subsidizing semi- or fully private "public" education models—from charter schools and vouchers to schools operated by for-profit companies and even the Department of Defense—has resulted in the solidifying of *choice* as a rationale for public education. This move is paralleled by a proliferation of unelected boards of education, mayoral takeovers of public school districts, weakened teachers' unions, and other attacks on modes of democratic participation. Increasingly, schools are presented as niche market options for consumers, and market metaphors are ascendant. Teachers are urged to use "best practices," measure "inputs and outputs," and "standardize" everything. These directions, when combined with the No Child Left Behind (NCLB) Act's emphasis on reading and math, have weakened many schools' support for the arts. The bottom line is that there is little room in these directions for an education that assumes the intellectual and creative capacity of all participants, with time for research and practice, jolts and tangents, play and experimentation, and a context-responsive curriculum that extends beyond the classroom, whether arts-infused or not. A standardized curriculum is inflexible; it can't respond to current events or artful explorations, and we think it's safe to say it generally brooks no velvet vulvas. But the velvet vulva and her sisters—from invitations to touch, listen, share, dream up, and relate in new ways, to bubble-lettered protest prints, videos shared in lunchrooms, and incantatory appreciations of hips and menstruation—are what will enable us to imagine and build our way into a future we might actually want to live in together.

CONCLUSION

The architect Louis Sullivan encouraged us to "Remember the Seed-Germ." Educators and artists alike are implicated in this charge: remember the essential core, the deep truth, the right doing of creating and of teaching. Art, planted in the field of education, is that seed—like a plant growing up through concrete, it will prevail; it will crack your classroom open, if you take it slow, allow the action, and let yourself be surprised. Art offers these tools and many others. Use them to make possible a rich and wholly humanizing education and life, for yourself and every child you teach.

DISCUSSION QUESTIONS

1. Assess: What are your own creative interests and practices? Do you make pickles or knit scarves? Design Web pages or garden plots? Attend gallery openings, paint portraits, work wood, or slam poetry? List five (or more) ways you can connect these capacities to your classroom.

2. Imagine: This chapter proposes taking it *slow*, keeping it *active*, and enjoying *surprise* in teaching. Can you think of ways these qualities could be teaching goals? What would you add to this list?

3. Challenge: Are there things you fear about bringing contemporary art, with all its unpredictability, oddness, and openings into nonnormative lives and goals, into your classroom and school? What pre–"shocking art" steps could you take to get ready?

FURTHER READING

Arendt, Hannah. 1968. *Between Past and Future: Eight Exercises in Political Thought.* New York: Penguin.

Bell, Clive. 1914. *Art.* www.csulb.edu/~jvancamp/361r13.html#Bibliography.

Clifton, Lucille. 1987. *Good Woman: Poems and a Memoir 1969–1980.* Brockport, NY: BOA Editions.

———. 1991. *Quilting: Poems 1987–1990.* Brockport, NY: BOA Editions.

Cochran-Smith, M. 2004. *Walking the Road: Race, Diversity, and Social Justice in Teacher Education.* New York: Teachers College Press.

Eno, Brian, and Peter Schmidt. 2009. *Oblique Strategies.* www.rtqe.net/ObliqueStrategies/.

Gayles, Gloria Wade. 2003. *Conversations with Gwendolyn Brooks.* Jackson: University Press of Mississippi.

Gladwell, Malcolm. 2008. *Outliers: The Story of Success.* New York: Little, Brown.

Greene, Maxine. 1995. *Releasing the Imagination: Essays on Education, the Arts, and Social Change.* Hoboken, NJ: John Wiley and Sons.

Holloway, Debra, and Margaret LeCompte. 2001. "Becoming Somebody! How Arts Programs Support Positive Identity for Middle School Girls." *Education and Urban Society* 33: 388–408.

Horton, Myles. 1990. *The Long Haul.* New York: Doubleday.

Janfamily. 2005. *Janfamily: Plans for Other Days.* London: Booth-Clibborn Editions.

July, Miranda, and Harrell Fletcher. 2009. Learning to Love You More. www .learningtoloveyoumore.com.

Kelley, Robin. 2002. *Freedom Dreams: The Black Radical Imagination.* New York: Beacon.

Livingstone, Joan, and John Ploof. 2007. *The Object of Labor: Art, Cloth, and Cultural Production.* Cambridge, MA: MIT Press.

Featuring seventeen essays and portfolios and projects by artists including Nick Cave, Ann Hamilton, Darrel Morris, Pepón Osorio, and more, this publication explores the personal, political, social, and economic meaning of work in the context of art and textile production.

Morris, William. 1883. *Art Under plutocracy.* www.marxists.org/archive/ morris/works/1883/pluto.htm.

Mortier, Gérard. 2009. *Art as Political Manifesto.* www.ispa.org/index.php/ resources/ideasexchange/65-mortier.

Paley, Nicholas. 1995. *Finding Art's Place: Experiments in Contemporary Education and Culture.* New York: Routledge.

Robinson, David. 1990. *SoHo Walls: Beyond Graffiti.* New York: Thames and Hudson.

Salas, K. 2004. "How to Teach Controversial Content and Not Get Fired." In K. Salas, R. Tenorio, S. Walters, and D. Weiss, eds., *The New Teacher Book: Finding Purpose, Balance, and Hope During Your First Years in the Classroom,* 127–132. Milwaukee, WI: Rethinking Schools.

Sennett, Richard. 2008. *The Craftsman.* New Haven, CT: Yale University Press.

Vygotsky, Lev. 1925/1971. *Psychology of Art.* Cambridge, MA: MIT Press.

Walker, Sydney R. 2001. *Teaching Meaning in Artmaking.* Worcester, MA: Davis Publications.

This book offers ways to bring the meanings that are often the core of contemporary art to everyday teaching.

ALSO OF INTEREST

Art:21—Art in the Twenty-First Century. www.pbs.org/art21/series/index .html. This television series created by the Public Broadcasting Corporation focuses on contemporary art and artists in the United States. The series has a great website with teacher resources, and all episodes are available on DVD.

CHAPTER THREE

OUR COMMUNITIES DESERVE JUSTICE!

Social Justice Teaching and Community Building

O
UR WORK AS teachers is never neatly bounded—this classroom or this school, from eight to three or from nine to five—it's just not that simple or that straightforward. Teaching involves building dozens, even scores, of intense relationships that are not easily shut off like a faucet at the end of the workday; our focus on teaching carries over into every other aspect of our lives and becomes, then, something that's never very far from our thoughts. Furthermore, our students live in families, communities, towns or cities, a nation, and a country—and so do we. Our lives are of a piece; they aren't experienced in fragments and segments. When school is treated as an entirely separate event, a little torn scrap of the whole wide world, that treatment does violence to teaching and learning, to healthy development, and to life itself.

When we think of families and communities as a distraction or a distortion, a deficit or a danger, we cut ourselves off from our potentially fiercest allies and an overwhelmingly positive force for the education of the young. We choose to think of families as colleagues and accomplices, communities as partners and assets, and we start with a strong faith, based on long experience: all families want something better for their children, and every community wants outstanding schools. We urge you to embrace that faith, too: your teaching will be enhanced, not diminished, when you get this relationship right, when you open your eyes and your arms to the positive potential and the goodness to be found in families and communities.

People sometimes ask our advice on how to bring relevant or controversial issues into classrooms: the truth is that relevant and controversial issues don't need to be "brought in" at all—they are flooding into every classroom every day, flowing over the transom, and rushing through every open door and window. Classrooms are porous places, and kids walk in with their lives in their hands, inscribed on their faces, embodied in every inch of them: they already know that the country is at war; they know that people are dying unnecessarily; they already know much of the wonder as well as too much of the horror of the human condition. What they don't know, and what remains to be seen, is how the adults in their lives will respond to any of it.

School people too often spend unreasonable and excessive energy deflecting, denying, ignoring, misreading, punishing, and suppressing most of what the students bring, the substantial material that is right there in front of their eyes: "We'll cover that later (or next year or never)"; "That's not something we talk about in school"; "You're not old enough"; "Ask your mom or dad."

Kids get three messages right away (or in a few years): one, school may be necessary to some, but it's also irrelevant, boring, sometimes antagonistic, and largely beside the point; two, powerful and important adults are too frightened or too beat down, too stupid, or too disconnected to tell the truth; and, three, the world is a dangerous and hostile place—you'll get hurt and you'll get hard, and, furthermore, you're largely on your own—and so you must learn to assume the defensive crouch of the warrior as you negotiate your pathways into (or outside of) this society. As teachers we counter each of these messages with a pedagogy of love and truth-telling, connection and community, and an updated three R's: relevance, relationship, revolution. *This pedagogy is a form of teaching for social justice, which can be defined as the day-to-day processes and actions utilized in classrooms and communities, centered in critical analysis and action among all educational stakeholders—students, families, teachers, administrators, community organizations, community members—and dedicated to the creation of a more just, equitable, and recognizably human society.*

Focus point

In education we are flooded with rhetoric: "standards" and "achievement," "accountability" and "best practices." Over time (and with overuse and misuse), each of these terms becomes a meaningless cliché diminishing and eventually shutting down our ability to think clearly or critically about any of it.

We worry about a related problem: "social justice teaching" has been used so often in so many situations to reference such a wide range of adaptations and bearings and practices—including any instance in which a teacher simply talks about an issue that she guesses might be pertinent to her students—that the phrase itself has overrun its banks and risks being reduced to a slogan without substance, a weak trickle where there should be a raging river. Simply put, the rhetoric is becoming shallower and emptier; "social justice" is a popular buzzword in some circles, but it is easily co-opted and rendered toothless in many places, and in other places it is lifeless, dead on arrival, without either any critical edges or any tangible examples of how teachers might bring justice orientations to life within resistant or even hostile environments.

Teachers with a social justice orientation oppose in their classrooms the objectification of people—all the

Teaching for social justice means living up to the demands of teaching in and for democracy.

forces that transform people into things for use; we oppose violence in its many overt and hidden forms; we oppose discrimination and segregation and exploitation of people. We support kindness, cooperation, fairness, courage, independent thinking, peace, love, and balance. Social justice teaching lives out a kind of happy and hopeful opposition. Our work is explicit and intentional in its focus on changing both individuals and the collective conditions of our lives—classrooms, neighborhoods, cities, nation, and larger world. This requires us to include a serious critical examination of *power* as it relates to race, class, gender, sexual orientation, and disability.

To us teaching for social justice means living up to the demands of teaching in and for democracy. We return to the democratic ideal: we must value every person's life in our schools and our classrooms; we must recognize the dignity and integrity of each; we must embrace the idea that the full development of all is the essential condition for the full development of each (and vice versa).

This valuing of democracy has huge implications, of course, for educational policy: racial segregation is wrong; class separation, unjust; disparate funding, immoral. What justification can there possibly be in a democracy for the existence of one school for wealthy white kids funded to the tune of $30,000 or more per student per year, and another school for poor immigrant kids or the descendants of formerly enslaved people with access to less than $5,000 per student per year? How does anyone rationalize or even explain the existence of an overcrowded hundred-year-old school building that looks like a medieval prison with a rotting roof and a busted furnace down the road from a generously appointed campus containing well-maintained athletic fields and an Olympic-sized pool as well as a state-of-the-art physics lab in a building that looks like a palace for learning? That's the indefensible reality in Illinois and in every other state of the union, and it's a reality that offends the very idea that each person is equal in value and regard, reflecting instead the dreadful idea that some of us are more deserving and more valuable than others. It expresses perfectly the simple but crude and cruel message we send to children too often concerning social policy: if your family has money, access, social connection, and privilege, your choices and your chances will expand; if not, sorry, you're on your own. No wonder so many kids are so resentful so much of the time, so many in full-throated rebellion at society as they find it.

But in the concrete day-to-day life in classrooms, too, the democratic ideal has a critical—indeed, a central—role to play. Democracy is predicated on people's informed and thoughtful engagement in a shared political and economic and civic life, and the foundations of democratic engagement are built on *independent thinking* and *critical analysis.* It requires people who are capable of self-realization (reflecting on their lives and becoming more conscious) and, at the same time, full participation (inserting themselves as actors in society and in history). Schools have been important to the development of such people. Classrooms that prepare people for democratic living are led by teachers who take seriously the demands of democracy, and then structure opportunities for free and critical thought as well as deep engagement and even action. These things are, of course, always in contention, generally under attack from some quarter or another; participatory democracy requires a high level of vigilance and activity in its defense and in its enactment.

School has always been and will always be contested space: What should be taught? In what way? Toward what end? By and for whom? We talk of equity and access as we should, but there is more: What kind of education? Whose questions are encouraged? Whose inquiries pursued? At bottom, the struggle is over the essential questions: What does it mean to be human? What does it mean to be an educated person? What does it mean to construct a meaningful, purposeful, and valuable life in the world, here and now? What demands does freedom make?

Focus point

No society is perfect, and none is entirely perfectible. One thing that sets a vigorous democracy apart from a mock or formalistic or sham democracy is the willingness of its people to admit that there is serious and ongoing work to be done: injustices to be identified and overcome, imbalances to be corrected, freedoms and liberations to be sought. A more perfect union is always an aspiration and never a point of arrival—it has yet to be achieved. This is the wide and dynamic arena of teaching for social justice.

We live in a painfully serious time and a critical situation: the three evils that Martin Luther King Jr. identified and preached against—militarism, racism, and materialism—have intensified and entrenched themselves in the past half century. War is a constant feature of American life now. White supremacy has adopted "post–civil rights" rhetoric, while racial disparities in everything from health care to incarceration to access to education continue apace. Poverty is rampant as the gap between rich and poor deepens and widens. Consumerism acts as a drug habit we seem incapable of kicking even as we acknowledge that it is killing us, our friends and families, and the planet itself. Each of these "evils" diminishes all human beings, and each can be seen as a challenge we can choose to face and take on, as citizens and as educators. Finding ways to name the challenges in their various new forms and guises, to oppose them in innovative and effective ways, and to identify real alternatives demands that we move with a heightened sense of urgency.

To take one salient example that some of us have been grappling with for years: local, state, private, and federal entities have waged a forty-year urban renewal experiment (dubbed "Negro removal" by community activists from the start) that has resulted in mass displacement of communities of color from revalued inner-city areas. In Chicago, as part of the larger gentrification process, public school students have been steadily pushed into distinct although hidden tracks: college prep, low-wage service or military employment, incarceration, and dropouts. As schools become a key conduit by which to "sell" newly gentrified neighborhoods to affluent home-buyers, this whole process is put forward as a positive contribution to the life of the city.

Omitted from the official story is the fact that thousands of poor residents of color have been displaced in the name of "progress." Many children and youth are forced into overcrowded schools because their neighborhood ones have been closed to make way for schools of "choice" for the more prosperous incoming residents, or they leave the system altogether because their families, unable to find employment or afford escalating rent prices, are forced to move to one of the even poorer suburbs now ringing the city. Students are sorted and tossed out into the world to participate as the products of these tracks, their destinies determined and set as early as the third grade.

Now more than ever we need real talk and real action—something often referred to as **praxis**—if we are to rectify the current realities in schools. Teachers can, if we choose, move beyond rhetoric and toward the substance of social justice education by engaging students, families, community members, and community organizers to study and research the goings-on right outside the schoolhouse door, and to challenge through concrete initiatives the difficult, unjust realities of urban education. That kind of classroom and extracurricular activity could keep your teaching vital, timely, and exciting. It could also keep you viable in your places of employment, and at the same time provide opportunities to engage other teachers in the ongoing project of teaching for social justice by demonstrating the potential power of this approach to their students.

There are several questions that can help to frame our discussion:

Key concept
Praxis involves critical thinking, reflection, and analysis in order to name injustices or imbalances and is linked to actions designed to change the world.

- What **relevant** content and engaged practices
  can social justice educators introduce into their
  classrooms to ensure or encourage positive,
  thought-provoking, critical, and challenging
  learning environments?
- What **relationships** can teachers build with students, parents, concerned community members, and community organizers in order to
  learn from them as they cooperate to create
  such spaces? How can teachers incorporate parents and community members into the curriculum as authentic partners? How can these folks
  serve as the essential bridge for social justice educators to build critical consciousness in young
  people?
- How can educators identify and effectively **resist** a system that does not support young
  people critically analyzing their situations and
  working to change their conditions? How do
  we encourage **revolutionary** change—sweeping
  transformations within every individual as well
  as fundamental structural revolutionizing of entire systems?

Wrestling with these questions sets us on a course to
become outstanding educators—the kind of social justice teachers who are poised to learn from, by, and for the
people.

Every one of us, of course, experiences pressure and
constraints; we each feel some fear. If we act, what do we
risk? If we don't act, what do we risk then? If we weren't
afraid, what might we do? What do we need in order to
find the courage to get started? One thing is certain: if we
choose to close our eyes and turn our backs, if we fail to
take the situations of our students and their communities as acute and urgent, if we fail to align ourselves with
their needs and hopes and fears, then we have chosen to
contribute to their detriment.

BEWARE THE "DO-GOODERS"

Obviously we are opposed to the "commonsense" notion that individuals and groups external to the institutionalized school (parents, concerned community members, community organizers) need to be "managed" by professionals. This thinking is highly problematic, as it positions parents and community members as forces who will likely prevent us from doing our work well. Because they possess the potential to disturb our work, "management" entails the minimization of distractions from the goals set forth by the individual teacher, school administration, district, or legislature. Placing this in the context of race, class, and gender, the people in need of managing are often low-income/working-class, of color, and overwhelmingly female. Whereas traditional management rhetoric marks these groups as troublemakers and adversaries, we consider them critical allies, people whose energy and insights are essential in creating the micro and macro functions of a good classroom. *If you provide avenues for students, families, and community members to contribute in meaningful and substantive ways to the process of education, you can build a foundation that will extend and help to protect the integrity of your work in classrooms over the long haul.*

Focus point

There's a telling bit of satire from *MADtv* available on YouTube called "Nice White Lady," which sends up the typical trope of practically every teacher movie ever made. The opening scene is an urban classroom replete with tough teenagers lounging on desks cleaning their guns and sharpening their knives while the voice-over catalogues the dangers of city schools: out-of-control kids, incompetent teachers, parents who don't give a damn, communities in collapse. What can possibly save them? At this point the classroom door opens a crack, and a young, fresh-faced teacher peeks in. Hi, I'm Amy Little, her beneficent smile says, here to help. She looks like a lamb ready for the slaughter, and when a young

Latina woman with maximum urban attitude gets up in Amy's face, issuing a profanity-laced list of deficits and disasters in her own life, Amy shrinks in horror. But she recovers, and dramatically pulls out pad and pencil, hands them to the young woman, and says meaningfully, "*Write that down.*" Soon everyone trades their guns for pens, and Pulitzer prizes are surely just around the corner. Of course, the dreadful veteran teacher scorns her efforts as misguided idealism—I know you mean well, but these children are *minorities!*—but she reminds him that she's a nice white lady—Lady Bountiful in the classroom—and that her good intentions and her heartfelt desire to save the little natives are all it will take.

The Maori community activist Lilla Watson offers a pointed and powerful response to this kind of thinking: *if you have come to help us, she says, you are wasting your time; but if you have come because your liberation is bound up with mine, let us work together.* Similarly, Ella Baker, the great civil rights leader, told the college-educated volunteers pouring into Mississippi in 1964 to help with voter registration that they should understand they had much more to learn from the sharecroppers and peasants they had come to "help" than the rural people had to learn from them. Begin by listening, she advised, and paying attention to the extraordinary ordinary people. Patronizing beneficence is an anemic alternative to full regard, authentic identification, and day-to-day solidarity with people, and Watson and Baker are reminding us in part that transformation is never a one-way affair.

Focus point

The complicated and messy work of teaching for social justice involves building transformative classrooms that push the self-development of both students and teachers who are mutually engaged in a struggle to learn and to teach, to change themselves and simultaneously to change others, and indeed to change the world around them. Together they work to provide tangible examples of what justice might look like in classrooms and in our communities, and why we must become new people if we are to be worthy of the changes we want to make. In this work there's no productive role for "do-gooders," people who view communities as all-deficit sewers of pathological neediness waiting to be "saved" by the saintly teacher who "cares."

Some new teachers are inspired to organize a "social justice day" or to start a "social justice" project. This is not really the way to begin—it's too tepid, too flimsy, and too cosmetic. Crises are everywhere—war, financial collapse, economic depression, chronic underemployment, war on the poor, runaway incarceration, privatization of everything from prisons and police to parking meters and public education, skyrocketing health care costs—and crisis is the defining tenor of these times. As Nina Simone laments: "*Can't you see it? Can't you feel it?*"

A pedagogy for democracy and liberation—teaching for social justice—should not be conceptualized as something done on the side or reduced to an add-on: pep club, debate, 4-H, Social Justice Day. Enlightenment and freedom, justice and liberation—these are the heart of the matter in a democratic society, coloring every relationship, each instructional gesture, and the entire curriculum. It begins with paying attention, seeing your students fully and in context, seeing the world wide and wondrous and in need of repair, and then plunging in and getting busy.

THE PERSONAL IS POLITICAL

We embrace the idea that our work as teachers constitutes a deeply personal and political act, and that the two sides of that dialectic are in fact inseparable. Teaching is traditionally positioned as an apolitical occupation—more technical, less relational, entirely disengaged from social life, and therefore much less messy. If you come from a traditional teacher-training program (or even one of the zillions of alternative programs springing up everywhere), chances are that your studies contained few

Focus point

courses that encouraged the politicizing of teaching. *If most teachers had in-depth knowledge about political economy, race, class, gender/sexual orientation, and their relationship to K–12 content areas, our classrooms would look remarkably different than they do currently.*

Carter G. Woodson noted that the masses of African Americans, if educated about the realities in which they were forced to live out their lives, would become "unruly" or "ambitious to become free." This strikes us as a central requirement for teachers: truth-telling. Some may argue that these realities of life are beyond the scope of your classroom and thus counsel caution, urging you to stay away from any of this; we urge teachers (and encourage ourselves) to dive in full-on. No K–12 classroom or content area is outside the scope of the political act of teaching. Some of the most forward-thinking teachers we know, for example, come from the disciplines of math and science; they tell us that the math and science folks who don't feel like they can make the leap to education for social justice are simply making excuses.

We should be clear that when we state that teaching is political, we are not referring to partisan politics. Instead, we are speaking about systems of power that operate above and beyond political parties or electoral matters, systems that affect all of us as teachers and as persons occupying multiple social, cultural, economic, and civic spaces in the larger world. This points us toward awareness and even analysis of the surrounding community and its relationship to the city at large, the school's relationship to the central office, the central office's relationship to the state,

Cross-Reference For a parallel discussion of the political dimension of teaching, see Book I, Chapter 6.

the state's educational relationship to the federal government, and our relationships to the various members of the school's surrounding community as well as our individual relationships with students, parents, and colleagues.

In Chicago, community organizations, parents, and teachers mobilized against Chicago Public Schools (CPS) to prevent the closing of twenty-two schools for the 2009–2010 school year. Calling themselves the Grassroots Education Movement (GEM), they were able over a long and sustained struggle to get several schools removed from the "hit list" of closings.

Peabody Elementary was scheduled for closure for what CPS called "underutilization." This designation represented a range of infractions from student underenrollment to nonuse of empty spaces in the building. When the school community was notified of the impending death sentence, parents and teachers alerted a group of local university researchers, and the newly formed team uncovered a critical fact ignored in the initial CPS report: Peabody was one of the few schools in the entire system with the capacity to accommodate young people with severe disabilities. It was also one of the few schools recognized for being in full compliance with the Americans with Disabilities Act. Further investigation revealed that one space cited for nonuse housed a resource center for parents. This vital school challenged the traditional notion of management by affirming the role of parents as critical actors in the educational community.

In the end, CPS acknowledged that the data collected by the Grassroots Education Movement were valid, and relented, explaining that placing Peabody on the hit list was a "central office oversight." The group felt a bit like someone who'd accompanied a friend to the hospital and wound up having to alert the staff just before a surgeon removed her gallbladder that she had in fact come for an eye exam: on the one hand, great that you could help out; on the other hand, *what the hell?*

No K–12 classroom or content area is outside the scope of the political act of teaching.

EXTRA WORK/BETTER WORK

Any type of education for social justice will require work beyond the scope of the 8 a.m. start and the 3 p.m. finish. This is obvious to most teachers, but for those who don't already know it, there's no sensible way around it. Because this work runs counter to current trends in management and accountability, you will constantly have to balance your own values, and work with the requirements placed on you by your individual school, the district, and the state.

The balancing act will mean negotiating a multitude of constraints. For example, if you teach in a school that uses a scripted curriculum, some supervisory person may periodically come into your class to make sure you're on a particular page at some precise moment. Teachers in these instances are operating under duress. Some have embraced their extra work by deconstructing the script: breaking down the goals and objectives, they replan the unit, taking an issue and concern of their students and remapping it onto the curriculum unit.

One fifth-grade teacher in Los Angeles has become an expert at this. He was required by the district to use a scripted curriculum called Open Court. Included in the curriculum was a unit on a dog, the objective of which was to meet the state requirement that students demonstrate the ability to write a descriptive letter. Students were asked to describe the dog using particular descriptors (color, size, disposition, and action) and then write a set of questions about what they wrote. The idea was to get students to pose questions and offer answers using their own words.

Instead of using the unit on the dog—something boring to him as well as his students—the teacher asked his students to write a letter describing any issue or concern they were having in their own lives. One common concern was the fact that substitute teachers in the building often disparaged students in their words and their actions. Many talked down to students, telling ten-year-old African American and Latino kids, for example, that they would never amount to anything in life and were destined to become prostitutes and bums. Alerted to this and taking serious issue with it, the teacher decided to shift the letter-writing unit to address these concerns.

During the letter-writing exercise, he caught word of a meeting of the service workers' union. These were the people who performed the services for the building (cafeteria work, maintenance/custodial, groundskeeping). He approached one of the union stewards and asked if one or more of his students could express their concerns about the district at an upcoming union rally. The steward agreed, and two fifth graders read their letters as part of the rally to support service workers in the school.

This teacher deconstructed the goals and objectives of the scripted curriculum, created a unit centered on a real issue of consequence to the kids, and demonstrated how his students could meet (and exceed) the state standard. Throughout the process, the teacher accomplished several critical things with his fifth graders. One was that by taking the students' ideas seriously, he built a different kind of relationship with them. A second was that he took an important concern and, instead of deflecting or ignoring it, he turned it into a curriculum matter, demonstrating that we can all learn from things that are relevant to us. A third was that he showed that we can act on what we see and know and uncover, and play a part, then, in something larger and more important than the teacher's grade book. A fourth was that he revealed that we can empower ourselves in the process.

Relationship (love and trust). Relevance (truth-telling). Revolution (transformed sense of self and possibilities).

All of this important learning came from a creative teaching initiative in response to a somewhat silly and surely disconnected unit about a dog. If you can imagine the extra work and planning involved in pursuing this unit, you are well on your way to understanding what we mean by extra work.

On the community level, when we want new teachers to learn about the neighborhood, we encourage as a start something like a community walk: a group of teachers led on a tour by a trusted community member with the aim of getting folks to develop a stronger feeling of connectedness to their surroundings. This can be useful and, when done purposefully and well, enlightening. We know an entire school faculty that decided to go a step further.

At the Lawndale/Little Village School for Social Justice (SOJO), every summer presents a new opportunity to engage the communities of Little Village and North Lawndale, which are Latino and African American neighborhoods, respectively. There is a concerted effort by staff to be intentional about introducing themselves to the community; and because the school came into being through the efforts of community members (mothers and grandmothers) staging a galvanizing nineteen-day hunger strike, the staff is extremely clear on the importance of community inclusion in creating an educational environment that is critical, reflective, and geared toward consciousness-raising and action.

Because SOJO is a small school—one hundred freshmen are admitted each year, and the staff consists of only nineteen teachers—each teacher makes home visits to the families of entering freshmen the summer before school begins. Unlike schools where teachers rush in and out as an unpleasant formality, or where home visits seem like little acts of surveillance representing a form of punitive discipline (signing family contracts dealing with homework or potential discipline issues with students), the purpose of SOJO home visits is of a different order: to allow teachers to introduce themselves to the families of the new students, and to provide families with several points of access and a range of possible ways to be in touch. Building relationships. Becoming partners. Being modest and even humble in approach and stance.

This may sound simple, but it can be instrumental in establishing the relationship between families and staff. It's part of the extra work because traditional teaching tells us that these types of interactions are unnecessary.

SOJO teachers are also cognizant of the power dynamics in play during a home visit. Some households fear intervention by local, state, and federal agencies that may result in the separation of families, and may not want teachers to visit the home. Out of respect for their right to privacy, teachers should always be aware of this possibility.

Extra work of the type described here is also better work. It is not make-work, and it is not work in the form of a gut check or an unreasonable genuflection meant to prove your "commitment" or your worthiness. It is relationship building and truth-telling. It is critical and it is essential.

GETTING OVER THE "WHAT TO DO NOW" SYNDROME

The "what to do now" syndrome occurs when a teacher gets to the point where a curricular unit may have ended or a unit has finished earlier than planned, or he or she decided to go in another direction with the unit because it has flat-out bombed in its current state. When any of these scenarios happen, teachers often reach the age-old question: *what am I going to do now?*

This is especially important for social justice educators because your teaching will take on a life of its own, and your planning will be of a different type altogether. Instead of mapping entire units and assuming everything is set for the year, you will have to intentionally carve out time to develop your teaching while evaluating existing work and determining whether or not it's relevant, whether or not it follows the interests and questions of students, and whether or not it connects to deeper and wider ways of knowing.

Social justice teaching is not some postmodern free-for-all, but it does have the potential to take off in numerous directions; it is therefore imperative that you take serious time to organize what you do as a teacher. It's important to plan, adjust, and develop your units, your curriculum, and your teaching. One effective way to promote your work as a social justice educator is to demonstrate that skills are indeed being learned through the content and approaches you have chosen to employ. This is not about standardization of social justice curriculum, but rather about focusing attention on how to create, critique, and revisit relevant spaces that will allow students to make informed decisions about their lives and seize an education worthy of a free people. This can also be done in a way that includes community, as in the case in Textbox 3.1.

TEXTBOX 3.1

A science teacher we know developed a unit on a coal-fired plant in the neighborhood where his school was located. Using an organization in the surrounding community as an anchor, he was able to collaborate to create a series of projects and assignments with the aim of engaging students in a real-life issue. Through this collaboration, he and the students discovered that there had been a community push to close the plant that dated back almost thirty years. The community where the plant is housed (the Little Village community in Chicago) has one of the highest rates of childhood asthma in the United States. Coal emissions are directly correlated with respiratory problems, and students were able to identify quite personally with the issue. As the unit progressed, students went through a number of experiments to demonstrate the harmful effects of particle ingestion over time. With the help of the partnering organization, the Little Village Environmental Justice Organization (LVEJO), students were able to learn about current efforts to address environmental justice issues in the community. In addition to the initiative to close the coal-fired plant, LVEJO was involved with other projects, including a push to develop a park, renew a discontinued bus line, and develop a sustainable living corridor in the neighborhood. The class was able to participate in thinking through various plans of action to address these problems, and so the students learned skills while connecting to bigger issues and working for change.

continues

Even more impressive was what the teacher did in his evaluation process. After this unit was finished, he asked his students to evaluate the work and develop a list of what the next unit should be. During this evaluative time, he projected the state standards for science on a screen and took notes on students' suggestions. From these suggestions and notes, he developed ideas for the next unit and brought them back to the class. This developed into a student curriculum team that worked to plan the forthcoming units for the class. Planning in this sense is antithetical to how we were taught to develop lessons in teacher education programs—everything based on a hierarchy of knowledge and ignorance, teacher above student, the knower and the blank slate.

TRUSTING YOUR STUDENTS AND COMMUNITY

Relationship building is central to teaching. This is the process of getting to know your students, where they come from, and how they interact with the world. Critical to this process is getting to know ourselves as teachers. Teaching for social justice in this sense moves away from the anthropological notion of doing research "on" someone and turns the arrow inward to carefully think about what we do as teachers. Our reflections are critical in continually assessing what went well, what didn't, and what more we need to know and to do. By reflecting on our work as teachers, we take a step toward what it means to trust our students and the community.

During 2008–2009, a handful of college professors decided to dedicate half of their college courseload for the school year to teaching high school classes at SOJO. Because two of the professors were on the design team responsible for developing the school, they had established important relationships with community members. When the time came to turn in the final proposal to CPS, one of the stipulations was that the two professors would teach at the high school.

Since its opening in 2004, these two have team-taught courses with SOJO faculty and consequently established close relationships with the students. Through the process of fostering these relationships, they felt that they could challenge their students in a constructive way while preparing them for college and next steps after graduation. They decided that in order to make the students' experience most meaningful, they had to challenge their own thinking as to what level of work the students could handle. In creating their classes, they decided to modify two graduate-level courses that they hoped would speak to the issues and concerns of the community: they *trusted* their high school students to take on the rigors of graduate work.

In concert with the promise made to the community in the initial proposal, the professors decided to add another component to the courses: students were dually enrolled at a local university and at SOJO; they would create a college class that would take place on a high school campus. Upon completion of the course, the students were given college credit that would count as an elective at any university they decided to attend. This type of relationship would not have existed if it were not for the initial efforts of the community to create the school. In the same vein, the accountability of the professors to the community-driven initiative was a key to providing this type of innovation for high school students.

SEEKING POWER IN THE COLLECTIVE

Teaching should not be a solitary act, especially for teachers who have made a conscious decision to go against the grain of "standards-based," "value-added," "research-driven" education. Conventional wisdom tells us to shut our doors and keep what we do in our classrooms between us and our students. Although this may provide some small amount of initial protection, many teachers will tell you how this process has a very short shelf life. Teachers with closed classrooms sometimes burn out or leave the profession altogether; other times they find their passion being sucked out of them. Teaching in isolation can be a painful experience that creates anxiety and distrust in your abilities as a teacher.

One of the most important things you can do as a social justice educator is to find allies—other teachers, parents, and community members—who are interested in supporting your work. It's crucial to be proactive throughout your journey as a teacher. In many cases we wait until it's too late to mobilize our colleagues and comrades in support of our work. There is a lot we can do on the front end of our teaching to solidify the needed support for our work.

Locally and nationally, a number of teacher collectives have engaged the task of establishing networks. Central to their process is the sharing of resources with each other to develop curriculum and to organize with families and communities. This creates a support network of educators committed to creating viable spaces for young people to ask critical questions and develop strategies to address their concerns. These mechanisms are critical in your journey as a teacher.

By embracing the fact that we are constantly learning, one of the most practical steps you can take as a new teacher is to find the people in your building who have a good reputation for teaching. We don't care how "bad" your school may be; there's always at least one. Once you find those people, sit down and ask questions about how they see teaching and how they see their students.

Not sure how to identify the right teachers to talk to? Ask your students who they think is a good teacher. Ask them what this teacher does, and why they think the teacher is good. Remember, the content area doesn't matter so much. What you want to get from these teachers is how they understand their students, the larger community, and the politics of the place in which you teach.

Find allies— other teachers, parents, and community members—who are interested in supporting your work.

Cross-Reference For more on community building in social justice, see Book 4, Chapter 2.

Another step you can take is to find other new teachers in the building, folks who are anywhere between their first and third years of teaching. Contact them, invite them to a space outside of the school (homes are always nice), and do something relaxing—a potluck, cookout, or movie night. Also invite the teacher identified by your students as a good teacher. Ask that teacher to say a couple of words about the school and whatever he or she feels you need to know about the building. When you wind down in the evening, ask folks if they want to get together again. If you receive positive responses, you're on your way to developing a space where you are able to reflect on your work and potentially bring other teachers from your area into the fold. This only takes three things: *time, space, and the will to keep it going.* Over time you will recognize that these collective spaces are critical to your survival as a social justice educator.

At the community level, there are a couple of other steps you can take to make tangible connections. One strategy is to find the person in your building who has the deepest ties to the community. In many instances, this person may not be a teacher. It could be someone who works in the front office, a school engineer, a security guard, or a member of the custodial/maintenance staff. Many times these people are overlooked as integral components of a functioning school. If we're honest, we will submit that these folks are often the lifeblood of the building. Honoring this community knowledge is key. If you're a new teacher, introduce yourself and be forthright in your conversation. It's not a bad thing to say that you're not familiar with the neighborhood. You won't be condemned for that. The most important thing is to understand that you must be respectful of the spaces you are entering, just as you expect students to be respectful of your classroom.

We know of a number of teachers who have engaged in this type of process and established considerable contacts for themselves in the community. Once they found those individuals with deep and tangible connections to the community, they asked them about good places to introduce themselves to the community. These might include a church gathering, a staff meeting at a local community center, or a block club meeting. When these teachers introduce themselves, they thank the group for letting them speak, tell them that they're teaching nearby and are new to the community, and then leave their contact information. They also stay after the meeting is over to talk to people. Key to this interaction is accountability—if someone calls or e-mails about a question pertaining to the school or community, *call him or her back*. Your ability to follow through as a teacher is critical to your long-term credibility.

Most important to the whole process, you absolutely must not be patronizing or condescending in establishing these relationships. Humility is the key. It will be important to remember one of the central components of effective teaching: *admitting that you don't know everything but are willing to find out*. People will respect you more if you take this approach.

We make this point as authors because here is where the real issues come to the table. Many who read this book may be apprehensive to approach others because they are unfamiliar with group differences in regard to race, class, sexual orientation, or ability. Don't use this as a crutch—admit it and move forward. Yes, many of you might find it extremely uncomfortable at first, but if you foreground your actions with the conversation and understanding that you want the very best for your students, you will be fine. Don't try to be something you're not; nothing good comes from that. There will be some trial and error in the process, but it deserves a concerted effort. This is also part of standing up for education and justice.

CONCLUSION: DIVING INTO THE CONTRADICTIONS

We would be lying if we professed that social justice teaching is easy. In many cases it is the direct opposite.

Cross-Reference
For more on embracing and accepting contradictions, see Book 1, Chapter 1.

Some of our schools resemble prisons more than palaces of learning. Some students are required to wear drab uniforms; some schools reward teachers for enforcing discipline over instruction; and some principals can hover like wardens looking over the general population deck. In these situations, teachers operate under duress and isolation, and some folks still are required to administer tests that we know do absolutely nothing in a positive learning sense for our students.

There are also personal contradictions that arise when we contemplate the extra work we put toward attempting anything transformative in the classroom. We sometimes have to come to grips with the fact that our lesson didn't work one day, or that our students think we are the worst thing in the world, or that we took a shortcut where we shouldn't have. These become the difficult spaces where we have to admit to failure while simultaneously engaging our ability to self-correct.

Within these contradictions, we have to muster the courage to ask uncomfortable questions. In addition to engaging these issues from a macro level, we must embrace the personal level. We still should ask: Why do we go outside the traditional boundaries of teacher education and school-based instruction to do the work we do? Why is it important? Knowing what we know, what substantive changes will we make in our lives to lessen the contradictions and move forward in providing an alternative context rooted in critical analysis and action?

The answers are not simple. Nevertheless, we embrace the difficulties of teaching and make the conscious decision to engage our students in forward-moving ways that are built on healthy and respectful relationships, relevance, and revolution.

DISCUSSION QUESTIONS

1. Before the requirements mandated by standardized tests or scripted curricula, what skills and abilities are you trying to develop with your students? Choose one area where you think your approach to curriculum, teaching, and learning might not align easily with school or district mandates. What is the nature of the misalignment, and how will you practically and concretely navigate the tensions and contradictions?

2. How are you prepared to navigate the tension between what you are trying to do in your classroom and what is required by your school, district, or state in terms of requirements or standards?

3. Who are the people inside and outside of your school who can support you in this process?

4. In what tangible ways are you engaging community concerns in your daily instruction?

FURTHER READING

Kozol, Jonathan. 1980. *Children of the Revolution.* New York: Delacorte Press. Though this book is out of print, you may find a used copy. It is an interesting account of Cuba's educational system after the revolution in 1959. Most notable is the ideology of free public education for all.

Oakes, Jeannie, John Rogers, and Martin Lipton. 2006. *Learning Power: Organizing for Education and Justice.* New York: Teachers College Press. This excellent book documents the partnership among university researchers, classroom teachers, and community organizations in the fight for justice and equity in California schools.

SUGGESTED RESOURCE

National Network of Teacher Activist Groups (www.teacheractivistgroups .org). This lists a number of teacher-based organizations across the country that focus on issues of social justice in communities and schools. Links to groups like the New York Collective of Radical Educators (NYCoRE), Association of Raza Educators (ARE), and Teachers for Social Justice (TSJ) are on this site, along with examples of curriculum and community initiatives.

CHAPTER FOUR

RESISTING THE PEDAGOGY OF PUNISHMENT

H OW WE NEGOTIATE and work through conflict—in our classrooms and communities—will increasingly define our democracy. Do we always lock people up? Do we respond to violence with violence? Do we necessarily isolate from our communities those who break the law? Working in communities to name and interrupt the militarization of our public schools is one possible route to challenge this growing public pedagogy of punishment.

THE PEDAGOGY OF PUNISHMENT

Residents of the United States live in a moment of unprecedented detention—the country accounts for less than 5 percent of the world's population but holds nearly 25 percent of the world's incarcerated people. At the start of 2008, the U.S. prison system held 2,319,258 men and women—one prisoner for every 99.1 adults. If those on parole or probation and those housed in jails or immigration detention centers are included, that number skyrockets to over 8 million. Our expanding prison population is not the result of increased lawlessness in our communities, but rather of national "tough on crime" policies: three-strikes laws, mandatory minimum sentences, the "war on drugs," increased power of prosecutors to try youth as adults. This ratio of incarceration indicates that the government is not "downsizing"; instead, it is increasingly regulating the lives of poor people, in particular African Americans, Latinos, and Native Americans.

The U.S. prison nation has been achieved *in public* through the passage of "tough on crime" legislation. Increasing state tax dollars now fund incarceration, not education; more prisons have been built in the past twenty years in the United States than new public colleges or universities. Dwindling state resources are funneled to policing, not to health care or housing—all in the name of *safety* and *security*. The collateral consequences of the previous two decades of expensive and expansive "tough on crime" policies have meant that U.S. residents have been taught that the military and prisons make our communities safer, that there are "bad" people out there who must be isolated and punished (not rehabilitated), and that retribution (not transformation or restoration) is the only kind of justice in town. By adulthood, most of us are well schooled in this ideology—a set of ideas we think of as the pedagogy of punishment.

The pedagogy of punishment is not confined to recycling dominant myths about what makes our communities or classrooms more secure. It affects all manner of policies—rarely is adequate funding for public education

TEXTBOX 4.1

To learn more about prisons, consider reading Angela Davis's *Are Prisons Obsolete?* Also check out organizations that work specifically on challenging public policies that enhance the pedagogy of punishment, such as Education Not Incarceration (http://ednotinc .org/).

raised as a sensible solution to school safety issues; in contrast, zero-tolerance policies are often proposed and accepted. The pedagogy of punishment extends to naturalizing future pathways for too many in our classrooms and communities—it makes it normal, and even sensible, that a thirteen-year-old's career aspirations would be to wear the uniform of a prison warden. The pedagogy of punishment schools us into unquestioning acceptance of the fact that millions of us are relegated to the enforcement and punishment economy. From the fronts of Iraq and Afghanistan to the tiers at Cook County Jail, from the Rio Grande to the South and to the west side of Chicago, violence and detention are always a growth industry: police officers, prison guards, mall cops, border agents, bail clerks, police dispatchers, court stenographers, jail doctors, Immigration and Customs Enforcement (ICE) translators and agents, weapons and punishment manufacturers/distributors, corporals, prison social workers, airport security staff, sergeants, truancy officers, private security guards.

As much as we may wish it were so, schools are not outside the punishment economy.

Laboring in jobs and in contexts that are premised at least *implicitly* on humiliation and the meting out of pain, and *explicitly* on isolation, exclusion, and therefore the dehumanization of people, triggers new relational pathways—rehardwiring ways of seeing and knowing—and subsequently poisons our communities and the very basis of democracy. Relying overwhelmingly on strategies for security and safety that augment our prison nation entraps larger and larger segments of our country's inhabitants—and this is literally a dead end for us all. As much as we may wish it were so, schools are not outside the punishment economy. We prepare our students for the world of work, and while there are few living-wage jobs as poets or muralists, La Migra is always hiring.

It is uncomfortable to even think that teachers could be added to the list of recruiters and employees in our permanent punishment and war economy. You joined

Everyone should have an equal opportunity to be remade by the power of poetry, maps, literature, quadratic equations, and physics.

teaching for some of the same reasons we did—for a paycheck, of course, but also because you believe in the reality that every person is valuable and that each of us can learn. Everyone should have an equal opportunity to be remade by the power of poetry, maps, literature, quadratic equations, and physics. The communities you want to live in are like the ones we work to build—where love struggles to be the center, gardens grow, and the desk chairs are not bolted to the floor in rows. You signed up to teach, to learn, to love—not to be a cop, a warden, or a parole officer. The futures you dream up for your students do not involve standing on either side of a border, a cell, or a gun.

Yet the reality is that schools play an instrumental and increasing role in advancing a pedagogy of punishment. As teachers, we need to see it, analyze and understand it, and then resist the whole of it—underlying assumptions, veiled meanings, explicit practices, *all of it*. We cannot afford to see our schools as outside of, or somehow protected from, a world where we have naturalized violence, isolation, and punishment as *public* responses to conflict of every kind.

Even with the best of intentions and the most progressive pedagogical visions, the communities we build in our classrooms are lovingly and chaotically effervescent, and classroom management techniques eventually fall flat. There is conflict in every relationship and community, and so in every classroom. Despite the messages we may receive as teachers, this is no personal failure on our part—this is life. And yet what snaps into place to manage every conflict in our schools is this ready-and-waiting pedagogy of punishment: detention, lockdown, isolation, time served. Why is this the default position, patiently waiting and then sprung into place at a moment's notice? This is a question for teachers in classrooms, for students, for the public, and for governments.

Focus point

For us, this is one of the centers of social justice teaching: linking our practices of discipline in schools to larger ques-

tions about how to address conflict—questions that circulate around and through our schools, our global communities, and through each one of us. Conflict is not solvable, avoidable, or *manageable*, so how do we live with conflict—as teachers, lovers, neighbors, nations?

We have no miracle cures. Instead, we offer to illustrate the critical importance of teachers working to turn away from a punishing logic: to *not* seek out the state in times of crisis; to *not* ask people and systems external to our intimate communities to discipline and regulate us when, inevitably, we and others do screw up. Not turning to the state means challenging the commonsense notion that punishment, isolation, and deprivation follow from crime or wrongdoing. We must work in schools to organize ourselves so that these are not the only choices available. We have strong foundations of resistance to draw from, and we have many allies. Challenging the militarization of schools offers us an opportunity to do this work. We must imagine, invent, and practice other responses to conflict. Our lives depend on it.

We juxtapose the pedagogy of punishment with **restorative justice.** Instead of seeking to punish, the restorative justice model asks how the perpetrators of harm or violence can be accountable to the communities and individuals who were hurt. How can relationships and communities be restored? How can we build systems of community accountability?

In 2007, Chicago Public Schools (CPS) eliminated zero-tolerance discipline policies and placed "restorative justice" in its Student Code of Conduct. Zero-tolerance policies were responsible for disproportionately suspending and expelling youth of color from the school system. Restorative justice, with peer juries and youth- and community-led mediations, opens the door to allow alternative models of justice to flourish in our schools and to rebuild our communities.

The move toward restorative justice in schools is just one example of efforts that push back against the pedagogy

We must imagine, invent, and practice other responses to conflict. Our lives depend on it.

Key concept *Restorative justice is a system that recognizes that our justice system is centered on retribution, and that this does not develop our participatory democracy.*

TEXTBOX 4.2

To learn more about the criticisms of zero-tolerance policies, read Russell Skiba's *Zero Tolerance, Zero Evidence: An Analysis of School Disciplinary Practice* (2000), available at www.indiana.edu/~safeschl/ztze.pdf, and *Zero Tolerance: Resisting the Drive for Punishment in Our Schools*, edited by William Ayers, Bernardine Dohrn, and Rick Ayers (New York: New Press, 2001).

Cross-Reference See Book 4, Chapter 6 for a related discussion of pedagogy and punishment.

Focus point

of punishment. Another material starting place to critically engage the pedagogy of punishment—for action, education, and dialogue—is to challenge the military's expanding presence in our schools and communities. Schools are *public* institutions that tenaciously and fiercely remake democracy. Challenging the militarization of our public school systems forces us to name our increased reliance on the pedagogy of punishment and the de facto assumption that the futures available to our nation's poorest youth are life in a prison cell or life in a uniform. Forget doctor, lawyer, artist, poet, beekeeper—the future for too many is conscripted and narrowed instead of widened and deepened through public education. *Interrupting and challenging the militarization of public schools also require us to fundamentally challenge and change ourselves—our taken-for-granted notions of what constitutes discipline and order, power and participation.*

In July 2009 the National Network Opposing the Militarization of Youth (NNOMY), an organization affiliated with approximately 150 local groups across the United States, hosted a meeting in Chicago to share strategies on counterrecruitment. Over three days, hundreds of community groups, youth, educators, and parents gathered to exchange tools, curricula, and ideas for local work. With sessions such as "Working from the Top Down: Changing School Board Policies," which documented how coalitions in Seattle and Los Angeles changed school board policies to restrict recruiters' access to middle and high schools, and "Alternatives to the Military," which offered strategies from campaigns in North Carolina and California to provide urban and rural youth access to career and educational alternatives to the military, the weekend was full of examples of how to build democratic, nonmilitary life pathways for all youth inside and outside of the classroom.

The 2009 NNOMY conference is just one indication of a growing movement led by youth, teachers, and parents that is challenging the militarization of our schools. The focus of this emerging movement is that public education in a democracy must remain a civilian matter, and that the values of education in a democracy—free thought, initiative and creativity, cooperation and dialogue—are in conflict with the military goals of hierarchical command and control, unquestioning obedience, and uniform conformity. Assuming a military force is needed in a free society, such a force should be based necessarily on (1) principles of nonaggression and respect for human rights; (2) fairness, honesty, and equity as basic terms of participation; and (3) open, full, and ongoing discussion at all levels of society concerning the role we expect it to fill and our collective priorities for its deployment. Without this, allowing the military access to proselytize and recruit the young is a kind of abuse.

Textbox 4.3 shows some current examples of communities resisting the militarization of public schools. *Educators have been and continue to be at the forefront of this work for change because we know what works to sustain flourishing communities and to build strong participatory democracies:* employment for all, including youth, that is not dehumanizing and that earns more than a living wage; a good public transit system; parks with trees; a kitchen for each of us with delicious food, books, music, and light. Democracies are only sustainable in the long run when schools and colleges are full, prisons and jails are empty, and the military is a minimalist, minor, and fully accountable institution.

Focus point

TEXTBOX 4.3

- San Francisco's Board of Education voted in 2006 to eliminate Junior Reserve Officers' Training Corps (JROTC) programs from its schools through a several-year phase-out. "It's basically a branding program, or a recruiting program for the military," said one San Francisco school board member before the vote (Tucker 2006, 19). Acknowledging that JROTC offered desirable things to students and families, the San Francisco board decided to develop and pilot new non-military-based programs to address those same interests. San Francisco's board subsequently voted that its public schools could not offer physical education credit for JROTC programs—a move predicted to end JROTC in San Francisco (Asimov 2008).

- Building on the work in San Francisco, the Association of Raza Educators (ARE) in 2009 called for the removal of JROTC programs in Los Angeles schools. The Los Angeles Unified School District (LAUSD) found that JROTC did not improve attendance, grade point averages, advanced placement course enrollment, or college-going rates. Citing the budget crisis in California that promised potential cuts to public education, ARE documented that LAUSD spent $3,863,247 on JROTC salaries in 2007 and argued that this money could be better spent by teachers to promote some of the same goals that JROTC claims to represent—leadership, college readiness, and more—without the military theme.

- In San Diego, California, a concentration of military might and border concerns, the Education Not Arms Coalition of youth, parents, and educators recently spent a year and a half securing a ban on rifle training on high school campuses. As Jonathan Flores, a student at Lincoln High (where there had been a free rifle range installed by the military), stated to the school board at a public hearing: "A school that teaches students to shoot weapons seems clearly ironic. Our books are the ultimate weapon to succeed, not guns. I also expect the board to uphold the idea that *no* guns in school means *no* guns in school!"

continues

> • Parents, students, teachers, and peace activists, notably the Mid-South Peace and Justice Center in Memphis, Tennessee, are publicly organizing and challenging the mandatory use of the four-hour Armed Services Vocational Aptitude Battery test for all juniors and seniors in the Memphis school district. In a school district where students need a note from parents to join the track team or the school band, data from this test are turned over to the armed forces and used to target youth military recruitment.

Parents, educators, and youth across the United States are taking action against militarization *in* and *out* of public schools. We are concerned about what educators can do to prepare students for peace, not war, and for democratic living grounded in reflective social justice practices, not for a barracks life punctuated by passive obedience and conformity—the hallmarks of every authoritarian regime throughout history.

Challenging the militarization of public education provides a rich illustration of justice work in education. Antimilitarization organizing in public schools requires bridging work across communities—students, staff, teachers, and parents. It is multidimensional because change must encompass policies at the district and school levels as well as curriculum development in the classroom. The work demands coalition-building because individuals and communities—including the working poor, African American, Native American, Latino, feminist, and/or lesbian, gay, bisexual, transgendered, and queer (LGBTQ)—have radically different histories with the military institution. Building justice movements involves learning, honoring, and working with these histories and struggles, and recognizing that contradictions will be a part of the work. Reflecting on antimilitarization work in education offers an example of these varied

TEXTBOX 4.4

For valuable insight into educator/activist lives, consider reading *Living for Change: An Autobiography,* by Grace Lee Boggs; *Anna Julia Cooper, Visionary Black Feminist: A Critical Introduction,* by Vivian M. May; *Citizen Teacher: The Life and Leadership of Margaret Haley,* by Kate Rousmaniere; and *The Long Haul: An Autobiography,* by Myles Horton.

facets of working for change and of the magnitude of being in it for the long haul.

Resisting the militarization of public education demonstrates, like all labors for social justice in education, that the critical issues we face in our classrooms and communities are interrelated. Although the militarization of our public schools is the "on the ground" problem that many educators, youth, and parents organize against, the militarization of our public schools is intimately related to the expansion of our increasingly punitive society and the pedagogy of punishment. Social justice work in education, by definition, means working hard to understand local issues in schools and classrooms, but also being able to name, explore, and resist the conceptual underpinnings of these local practices. Exploring the militarization of schools must move us to think about discipline.

THE MILITARIZATION OF EDUCATION

As a concrete example of the pedagogy of punishment, we start with where we are located: Chicago. Chicago has the most militarized public school system in the nation; the public school systems of other large and largely black and brown urban centers in the United States, including Philadelphia, Atlanta, and Oakland, follow closely behind. Nearly 10,000 students in Chicago participate in

the Junior Reserve Officers' Training Corps (JROTC) program—beginning as early as the Middle School Cadet
Corps program—and some 2,400 are enrolled in one of
Chicago's six public military high schools and military
schools within schools. Chicago is the only city in the nation to have academies representing all the branches of the
military. With false promises of enormous cash-signing
bonuses or free college tuition, distribution of free "first-
person shooter" video games, and seemingly unfettered access to places where children congregate (including
schools) without the presence of parents or guardians, the
military is enhancing its youth-recruitment campaigns—
and public education is a logical step.

Chicago's public military academies—along with
other schools offering limited curricula, such as vocational education schools, education-to-careers (ETC)
academies, and schools using only scripted Direct Instruction lessons—have been placed primarily in low-
income communities of color. In contrast, schools with
rich offerings—including magnet schools, regional gifted
centers, classical schools, International Baccalaureate (IB)
programs, and college-prep schools—have been placed
in whiter and wealthier neighborhoods across Chicago.
In other words, it's no accident where military schools
are situated and who is likely to attend them.

This policy of Department of Defense (DOD) public
military schools has been implemented through civilian
arms. In 2001, Chicago's mayor Richard M. Daley, in a
letter to the editor, commented approvingly on an article
in an online journal, *Education Next*, in which Jerry
Brown, who was then mayor of Oakland, California, offered his rationale for public military academies. Daley
congratulated Brown's efforts to open a public military
high school in Oakland and explained his own reasons
for creating military schools in Chicago:

We started these academies because of the success of
our Junior Reserve Officers Training Corps (JROTC)

program, the nation's largest. JROTC provides students with the order and discipline that is too often lacking at home. It teaches them time management, responsibility, goal setting, and teamwork, and it builds leadership and self-confidence. (Daley 2001)

Order and discipline, time management, and teamwork are goals the JROTC program always highlights, whereas the process through which these goals are acquired—weapons assembly, marching in military formation, memorizing ranks and hierarchies and battle plans—is conveniently left out. But let's not be fooled: programs like JROTC have always been about recruitment.

This push to build DOD public schools in urban centers is not a new practice. After the start of war in Europe in 1914, calls increased for universal military training in public schools and colleges as a way to resolve perceived social problems, including "moral rot" associated with increased national wealth, a rise in the number of immigrants (who were seen as insufficiently loyal), and growing demands by labor, especially through strikes. The military and a militarized education were prescribed as cures for "the hollow-chested boy" and the suspect masculinity of the immigrant, who could develop "a manly readiness" through participation in school-based drills and army training (Bartlett and Lutz 1998, 122, 123). In 1916, Congress passed the National Defense Act, which approved the establishment of JROTC units in public high schools, and from the start its primary purpose was understood as ideological, not vocational or educational.

Focus point

All the slick talk about access to education, leadership skills, jobs, and more belies the real rationale for JROTC programs and Department of Defense–run public schools: because so many of our other public systems abjectly fail our communities. From our work in schools, we know all too intimately that our public schools do not offer an equal education. Some kids get sculpture and Web/broadcast journalism while others get vocational math, auto mechanics, and cosmetology. Going to college or to graduate school is prohibitively expensive, yet a high school education cannot get you a minimum-wage job. Our immigration system criminalizes too many youth and renders them ineligible for higher education or the general labor force. Just as prisons trap our homeless and mentally ill, the ranks of our military surge with poor youth and those shut out of other democratic possibilities. It is what poor men and women do.

Those looking to maintain and develop military programs in public schools know this and subsequently cloak their military aims. JROTC programs teach *discipline*, and DOD schools offer *leadership opportunities*. Rarely are these DOD schools and programs discussed in military language. This rhetoric is a turnoff. Instead, what is offered are clean hero stories full of images like those in the "Army of One" recruitment ads deployed before youth-targeted films: shiny soldiers saving grateful women and babies, youth in crisp uniforms jumping from planes, fresh-scrubbed faces hovering over flickering technology. And for some youth, given the dearth of humanizing employment opportunities in urban contexts (and given that these youth are generally deprived of access to meaningful college pathways), who wouldn't be swayed by this marketing? Join the military to become a hero and get a valued and respected job, or stay in your 'hood and work double shifts at Popeye's for $7.75 an hour?

The expansion of the military into public education is about recruitment, but it is also about acquiescence to the militarization of our everyday lives. By accepting the military in schools, we also tacitly accept the myth that violence and punishment make our communities and schools safer. Militarization is a manifestation of the pedagogy of punishment, and the markers of this militarization are everywhere: expanding borders and detention centers, increased surveillance of public places, antiloitering laws and curfews for youth, on-site police detachments in public high schools, cops armed with assault rifles, and Amber Alerts as the looping public soundtrack. These state efforts to "defend" our communities are always more of the same. Because schools are central components of our communities and our democracies, resisting militarization and the pedagogy of punishment in schools is imperative.

WHAT YOU CAN DO: CURRICULUM AND COMMUNITY ACTION

Focus point

Our strength is that we have deep and wide foundations of democratic resistance, and teachers have always been at the forefront of social change work, in particular concerning the militarization of our communities. Our work as teachers in schools has always been to recover what is fundamentally public, common, peaceful, and democratic. This is never settled terrain; it must be constantly worked for and created within each generation and community. The National Education Association (NEA) took a strong stand against universal military training at its 1915 meeting but reversed its position later with a conflicted statement that "the training should be strictly educational . . . and military ends should not be permitted to pervert the educational purposes and practices of the school" (quoted in Bartlett and Lutz 1998, 124). Since the inception of JROTC, groups of parents, students, and educators have resisted its imposition in widely publicized events. In 1929 the *New York Times* published "United Parents Vote Against School Drill," documenting a parent group's unanimous vote against military drills in schools, and in 1945 the *Times* revisited the subject with "Debate Military Training: School Pupils Give Views at Panel in Times Hall."

Focus point

Intervening in the militarization of our public schools gives us the opportunity to discuss, in public, the very questions that are central to building sustainable and flourishing democratic communities: the roles of education in a democracy, the nature of childhood (and humanity), the role of war to "solve" violence and conflict and to achieve peace, and the fiction that citizenship and community (and adulthood and masculinity) are achieved through participation in a war economy. These questions, and others about the role of violence in struggles for justice, offer additional opportunities to discuss in classrooms the struggles of oppressed communities to sustain and even to refuse nonviolent strategies for change: Gandhi, Rosa Parks, Malcolm X, and Sylvia Rivera. These are questions that each generation must debate in public—and schools are one public place for these dialogues.

The New York Collective of Radical Educators (NYCoRE) curriculum, *Camouflaged: Investigating How the U.S. Military Affects You and Your Community*, offers educators tools for both inside and outside the classroom. Available through the NYCoRE website (www .nycore.org), *Camouflaged* provides lesson plans for a range of subject areas and grade levels. A media literacy unit asks students to examine a collection of military recruitment posters and multimedia recruitment products, from the war of independence to the current war in Iraq, for overlapping themes. The unit not only offers historical content knowledge but also supports the development of media literacy skills as students compare the messages of patriotism, militarism, and masculinity that are represented across different eras, and analyze how different racial and ethnic groups are targeted at different moments in U.S. history. A mathematics lesson plan asks students to use readily available numbers to calculate the real cost of war. For example, a word problem asks: "According to the National Priorities Project, as of January 2008 the cost of the War in Iraq was over $485 billion. If we stacked $1 bills, how tall would that be? Consider that the Empire State Building is 1,472 feet tall (including the antennae); would the money reach the top? Would it be taller?"

The worksheets included in this lesson ask students to engage in a number of calculations, but also pose a

number of additional questions: *What did you learn?*
What surprised you? The lesson plan thus stresses math
competencies while linking sociopolitical analysis to the
calculations that the students practice. What is the impact of this government expenditure on other facets of
their lives?

Edwin Mayorga, an elementary school teacher and author of the curriculum guide, explains the rationale behind the creation of *Camouflaged:*

> As educators committed to the creation of a more just
> world for young people to live in, we recognize that
> shaping schools into heavily shriveled and militarized
> contexts only further criminalizes youth and tracks
> youth solely into economic opportunities that maintain
> wars and prisons. As educators, we therefore work to
> provide educators and youth the curricular resources to
> analyze, interrupt, and transform the structures that op-
> press us all.

With worksheets, links to primary source materials, discussion questions, visual aids, and more, *Camouflaged* offers many places to infuse our curriculum with units that
have the potential to be transformative.

Many teachers have also worked with students to start
student-run social justice clubs. Meeting at lunchtime
and after school, students work on issues that affect
their community. At Chicago's Kelly High School,
which continues to be heavily targeted by military recruiters, students in the Social Justice Club organized to
visit classes across campus to educate their peers about
the recruiters and to distribute "opt-out" forms. If parents or guardians sign these forms, the military cannot
talk to youth without the presence of a parent or
guardian. These forms are supposed to be widely available in public schools, but all too frequently youth and
parents are not informed of this right. In the last few
years, because of the work of this club, almost half of

Kelly High students returned signed copies of the opt-out form.

The American Friends Service Committee (AFSC), a national organization, produces a number of tools—films, interactive websites, curricula, pamphlets, posters, brochures, and more—and often employs youth and veterans to organize counterrecruitment campaigns. The AFSC's *Do I Know Enough to Enlist?* materials are readily available in English and Spanish, online (www.afsc.org/Youth&Militarism/) and from any AFSC storefront office. *Questions for Military Recruiters*, a free download, is a palm card with seventeen essential questions for all youth to ask recruiters, including "How long is my enlistment commitment actually for?" and "Have you ever seen combat and do you think exposure to it is healthy for me?"

Schools in Chicago most heavily targeted by recruiters have also brought in interactive site-specific installations by the AFSC. *The Real Cost of War*, which is available to be exhibited in any school, addresses the financial and other burdens of living in the United States in a time of a permanent war economy. The AFSC recognizes that the real reason so many people join the military is financial—the poverty draft—and therefore provides materials that critique and break down these myths about the economic opportunities associated with enlisting. The committee also produces *regionally specific* resources to support alternative economic pathways, most notably magazine guides that outline how to secure employment and college access. Youth activities are offered to support youth as "peace recruiters": there are summer organizing camps, peace poster competitions, art classes, and more.

People in many communities use the AFSC's resources to sharpen and direct conversations specifically for educators. In Chicago in the summer of 2009, Teachers for Social Justice organized a forum on restorative justice. Approximately forty educators attended this session on a hot Saturday night in June. This forum led to the development of an ITAG, or Inquiry to Action Group, for which educators committed to eight sessions to examine what restorative justice could look like in their schools and classes. Facilitated by practitioners from a range of affiliated organizations and educators, these ITAG sessions include readings and are full of examples of how to start peer juries, develop conflict resolution skills, and more. This program culminated in comprehensive peace-circle training. An ITAG on restorative justice is one example of the many teacher-initiated possibilities for challenging the pedagogy of punishment by building in schools—through teachers—restorative justice capacities. Jonah Bondurant, a Chicago high school teacher, states why he and Sarah Atlas, another Chicago educator, started the ITAG on restorative justice:

> I got involved with organizing the restorative justice ITAG because I believe in change from the bottom up. Teachers and our allies, the parents and students, are the only ones who can re-make our education system and our society. Restorative justice offers a more spiritual and ethical orientation that I sometimes feel is lacking in social justice education. Also, restorative justice offers some concrete methods and approaches that teachers can implement themselves to reduce punitive punishment and referrals to law enforcement while also building community.

As Bondurant states, moving away from a pedagogy of punishment (and militarization) in schools also can move us to ask about a most intimate schooling practice: discipline. Discipline is too often the public sensibility used when expanding punitive systems for youth—from JROTC and public DOD schools to zero-tolerance policies and juvenile detention centers. *The kids are unruly, dangerous, and they need structure and discipline*—this is all too often the public message that surrounds the implementation of everything from metal detectors in schools to mandatory student uniforms. However, it's important to note that many school-based routes to developing discipline—art education (dance, music instruction, theater and performance, visual arts), sports and physical education, after-school activities and clubs from chess and debate to radio journalism, and much more—are not available equally to all youth.

In Chicago, for example, 20 percent of principals report that their public schools offer no arts programming at all, with children in low-income communities of color less likely to have school arts than students in wealthier, whiter neighborhoods (Illinois Arts Alliance 2005). It is vital that teachers and communities research and persistently ask, What kinds of discipline do the youth in my community have access to? In a 1916 essay in the *New York Times*, a school director, Dr. James Mackenzie, argued against the ROTC and in favor of discipline: "If American boys and young men lack discipline, by all means let us supply it, but not through a training whose avowed aim is human slaughter" (Mackenzie 1916, 16). Resistance to these narrow and unlovely definitions of discipline, spread throughout history, is ongoing.

Often, resistance comes first from our students. In a relatively affluent suburban Chicago school district, student Max Ellithorpe responded to the 2009 spring Military Appreciation Month at Highland Park High School by raising questions:

> I'm emailing you regarding the Military Appreciation Month at Highland Park High School. I understand the importance of supporting our troops, and recognize the appropriateness of devoting a month of appreciation. However, I think it is misleading for recruiters to come every day to our school and display large plasma TVs, video games, and fancy vehicles. As I've walked through school these days, and in conversations with fellow students and also some of my teachers, I've been a bit disturbed. At the main entrance for a few days, there was a

full-size cutout of an MP with an attack dog. In the library foyer there are pictures of coast guard officers pointing weapons at enemy boats. Every day I worry that more and more kids are lured in by these recruiters who glorify war by displaying hummers as well as popularized images of extreme fitness and combat. I understand that this month is meant to appreciate their service and their daily commitment. To be quite frank, I don't think Air Force members play "guitar hero" out of painted Humvees on a daily basis. I think it would be more appropriate to invite in a parallel table as well from Iraq Veterans against the War. While I'm sure that members of the military enjoy what they do and find time for fraternization and fun, many are emotionally and physically scarred in the process. This is just one idea to show an alternative but equally valid viewpoint. Perhaps we can work together to come up with more ideas to level the playing field.

Nancy Cruz, a former student at Mission High School in San Diego, started organizing with other students because they saw their school, attended primarily by low-income youth of color, actively targeted by military recruiters and because they felt they were being denied access to their dreams—to become lawyers, teachers, and psychologists. In a flyer distributed at the 2009 counter-recruitment conference in Chicago, she wrote:

> As students we took it upon ourselves to do what was right and let our principal, administration, parents, school board, and nation know what we think. We have petitioned, protested, walked out, leafleted, spoken to the school board, been interviewed by TV and radio, networked with other schools such as Lincoln High, and helped found the Education Not Arms Coalition.

Students like Max and Nancy are not just learning in the classroom; through their organizing they are acquiring skills in communication, political analysis, media literacy, and democratic participation.

TEXTBOX 4.5

Here are some general action steps we and others continue to take to challenge the militarization of public schools and to continue the daily work of building a sustainable participatory democracy. These are basic areas to start from. We know that coalition work and community building are, by definition, local and that there are no recipes for organizing. We offer places to start, questions to ask, and curricula to create. Building from the previous examples of NYCoRE, the AFSC, and the ITAG model, this is what we do:

- Partner with organizations such as the AFSC to get antirecruitment materials into your school. If the military is recruiting for the permanent war machine, our job is recruiting for full and raucous participation in the civilian democratic experiment. Organize visits to your classrooms from veterans' groups and youth organizers who are invested in Truth in Recruiting campaigns. You will never be alone in this work because so many are already working alongside you, including the AFSC.
- Educate ourselves, colleagues, students, parents, and communities about our district's parent/guardian opt-out policy. Parents/guardians have the right to be present when a military recruiter talks to their child, but they must typically sign a form requesting that they be notified when their child is contacted by a military recruiter. "Opt-out" limits the ability of recruiters to access youth. Circulate these forms, work within your school to create education campaigns about this process, and inform parents and students about their rights.
- Educate ourselves about our school district's written access policy for military recruiters. In Chicago, teachers, community members, and organizations worked to change the district's policy to require that recruiters notify principals when they arrive at any school grounds to recruit youth. The new policy states that recruiters cannot roam freely through the school. What is your district's policy?

continues

TEXTBOX 4.5 continued

- Engage our students in research and creative art projects that work to make visible and to challenge the pedagogy of punishment. What are the disciplinary policies and practices in your school and classroom? What are some alternatives? How much funding goes to prisons in your state? To higher education? Where are the Department of Defense programs in your school district? Youth and parents support these military programs because they provide concrete and needed resources. What are the reasons why youth at your school enroll in JROTC programs? Map the sports, music, and art programs at the schools in your area and compare them with the school and community support for JROTC programs.
- Research your school's and state's health, wellness, and physical education standards. In many schools, students get credit for participating in JROTC programs. Raise the question, why can students get physical education credit for participating in JROTC?
- Check out the peer mediation or restorative justice materials available in your community. Perhaps these resources are at the local law school, or maybe they are available through a religious or community-based organization. Get trained. Talk a friend from school into going with you. These programs offer a wealth of information—from networking with like-minded teachers to training on peer mediation and conflict resolution—and often resources and programs to divert youth from juvenile justice systems.

We challenge the punishing logic of militarization with our most powerful weapons: growth, love, community, generosity, and a profound belief in change. Love comes from and through community. Start a reading group. Grow a garden outside your classroom. Organize a queer dance party, a field trip, or a mural project at your school.

CONCLUSION

Teachers resisting the pedagogy of punishment inside and outside schools can't do it alone, so get with a posse. Link up with a community-based organization: your union if you are lucky to have one; your faith organization if its members think lovingly, generously, and expansively; and/or the folks on the block. You can find helpmates in the most everyday and unusual of spaces. One is too lonely for this work. As teachers, we all too often want to just shut our doors and think of our classrooms or even our schools as private spaces that we have some control over. A radical gesture, from the start, is to always consider these spaces as public and knowable, and to always use the term *ours* instead of *mine*.

The time won't ever be better to resist the pedagogy of punishment, and the stakes will always be high, so do something *in community*. Start anywhere; don't wait. As the poet Marge Piercy wrote in 1982, being of use when "the work of the world is common as mud" consists, in large part, of showing up and following through and, sometimes, getting out of the way. Changing institutions requires changing people—starting with ourselves—and this is about doing the difficult work to understand our "cop in the head" and our "cop in the heart," or how institutions and their corresponding regulatory practices live in and through each of us. How do we participate in reproducing or resisting the pedagogy of punishment in our lives? What do we bring into our classrooms unconsciously, from our own schooling and disciplinary histories?

Dig in, and don't mark your work by failures. Fear is difficult to interrupt. Transforming ourselves and our schools is the hardest work, because imagining and working toward a future where we do not rely on punishment means we need to remake many facets of our life while we live. And, yes, this is overwhelming, and that is why community is central.

DISCUSSION QUESTIONS

1. Make a list of all the ways the current wars affect you and the communities you work and live in.

2. What are your own experiences with discipline? How were you raised? How were you educated?

3. What organizations and groups are working to challenge the militarization of youth in your community? How can you connect and link your work within the school to their work?

4. Building from and beyond the suggestions in this chapter, what are two things you can do every day to challenge the pedagogy of punishment in your classrooms and in your school?

FURTHER READING

Asimov, N. 2008. "S.F. School Board Kills PE Credit for JROTC." *San Francisco Chronicle,* June 27, B1. Available at www.sfgate.com/cgibin/article .cgi?f=/c/a/2008/06/27/BAJ411FPOE.DTL.

Bartlett, L., and C. Lutz. 1998. "Disciplining Social Difference: Some Cultural Politics of Military Training in Public High Schools." *Urban Review* 30, 2: 119–136.

Bornstein, Kate. 2006. *Hello Cruel World: 101 Alternatives to Suicide for Teens, Freaks, and Other Outlaws.* New York: Seven Stories Press.
Offers youth and other readers an engaging self-help tour to living life outside the box.

Critical Resistance Collective. 2008. *Abolition Now!* Oakland, CA: AK Press.

Daley, R. 2001. "Correspondence: Military Academies; Do Teachers Matter?" *Education Next.* www.hoover.org/publications/ednext/3384806.html.

"Debate Military Training: School Pupils Give Views at Panel in Times Hall." 1945. *New York Times,* January 20. Available at www.nytimes.com/.

Ferguson, Ann. 2001. *Bad Boys: Public Schools in the Making of Black Masculinity.* Ann Arbor: University of Michigan Press.
Provides theoretical analysis of how race and masculinity interact with dominant school cultures to produce youth as deficient and "bad."

Illinois Arts Alliance. 2005. *Arts at the Core: Every School, Every Student.* www.artsalliance.org/ed_research.shtml.

Mackenzie, James C. 1916. "Can Schools Give Military Training?" *New York Times*, September 10. Available at www.nytimes.com/.

Pew Center on the States Public Safety Performance Project. 2008. *One in 100: Behind Bars in America 2008*. Washington, DC: Pew Center on the States. www.pewcenteronthestates.org/uploadedFiles/One%20in%20100.pdf.

Piercy, Marge. 1973. "To Be of Use." In *Circles on the Water: Selected Poems of Marge Piercy*. New York: Alfred A. Knopf.

Starhawk. 1993. *The Fifth Sacred Thing*. New York: Bantam.
A science-fiction novel that offers a thick description of communities struggling with nonviolent resistance to state and interpersonal violence.

Tucker, J. 2006. "San Francisco School Board Votes to Dump JROTC Program." *San Francisco Chronicle*, November 15, B1. Available at www.sfgate .com/cgibin/article.cgi?f=/c/a/2006/11/15/BAG2HMD46B1.DTL.

ALSO OF INTEREST

The film *All Quiet on the Western Front* (1930) represents trench warfare during World War I. Depicting the cost of war on all who serve, it suggests that wars produce only "losers," no winners.

ORGANIZATIONS FOR ACTION AND RESOURCES

American Friends Service Committee: www.afsc.org/Youth&Militarism/
Bus Riders Union: www.thestrategycenter.org/project/bus-riders-union
Critical Resistance: www.criticalresistance.org
Education for Liberation Network: www.edliberation.org/
Education Not Arms Coalition: www.projectyano.org/educationnotarms/
Education Not Incarceration: http://ednotinc.org/
Los Angeles School District Report on JROTC: http://cutjrotc.pbwiki.com/
   LAUSD-Report-on-JROTC
National Network Opposing Militarization of Youth: www.nnomy.org
New York Collective of Radical Educators: www.nycore.org/
Mid-South Peace and Justice Center: www.midsouthpeace.org
Teachers for Social Justice (Chicago): www.teachersforjustice.org/

CHAPTER FIVE

IMPROVING EDUCATIONAL POLICY

Reframing the Debate,
Reclaiming Public Voice

WE HEAR IT ALL the time: the work of teachers is exclusively the work that happens in classrooms. Let the principals worry about the school; let the parents worry about the community; let the elected officials worry about policies, laws, and the many reforms coming our way. Indeed, the advice often given to a new teacher is to just shut the door and do your own thing, make your classroom the space where you can really have an impact on the lives and learnings of your students. The value of independence, of course, should not be underestimated; the autonomy of teachers is necessary if we are to tailor our teaching to the diverse needs and capacities of our students, as well as to the unique contexts in which we find ourselves. Nonetheless, the work of teachers does and should extend far beyond the walls of our classrooms: we are members of the community, after all—in fact, of many diverse and overlapping communities—and of families and the whole

Teaching has long been integral to broader movements to change society.

society. We have a stake in the larger context and a responsibility to a wider public.

Teaching has long been integral to broader movements to change society and to make our world a better place for all. In the 1800s, Catharine Beecher was one of several prominent educators pushing forcefully for expanded educational opportunities for women and girls. In 1933, Carter G. Woodson published *The Mis-Education of the Negro,* in which he not only critiqued existing curriculum for its Eurocentrism and the many ways that it taught black students inferiority within the racial hierarchy of the United States, but also called on educators to raise critical consciousness among the nation's youth. Unions of public school employees, including the American Federation of Teachers and the National Education Association, marched shoulder to shoulder with national and local civil rights organizations during the black freedom movement of the mid-1900s. During the civil rights movement, activists and educators created "freedom schools" across the South and then across the nation, aiming to teach the next generation ideals of democracy as well as skills for social change.

Across the country today, a host of organizations call together teachers who are committed to equity and justice in public schools. These engaged activist-educators organize curriculum fairs, campaigns, meetings and forums, conferences and professional development events, and initiatives to change policy and the decision-making process. A group of teachers in one city organized to ban standardized testing in early childhood education as pointless at best, and likely destructive to student learning and development in most cases, and following a spirited campaign and the mobilization of parents, the district discontinued all K–3 standardized tests. Teachers in another city opposed the imposition of a specific basal reading program on all schools and won an initiative to allow teachers at the school level to choose the reading program that they thought best for their classrooms from three distinct alternatives reflecting different philosophies of learning. Teachers in a third district fought for and won the discontinuation of military recruitment in the district's high schools.

If teachers spend their time and energy grumbling instead of organizing, the one sure outcome will be the continuation of the status quo, including the existing inequities and injustices. If we work hard, get smart, mobilize and organize in the community, come together to speak up, and make our voices heard, teachers can become a powerful force for authentic and substantive school improvement. To get started and to get going, call together a few interested colleagues and check out one or more of these networks: Education for Liberation; the National Association of Multicultural Educators; the Association of Raza Educators in Los Angeles; Literacy for Social Justice in St. Louis, Missouri; the New York Collective of Radical Educators in New York City; Teachers 4 Social Justice in San Francisco (Pui Ling Tam, puiling@cessf.org); Teachers for Social Justice in Chicago; and Rethinking Schools in Milwaukee, Wisconsin.

Focus point

The historical role that teachers have played in social movements is important to contrast with the current initiative to minimize the impact teachers can have on public education. Often teachers are not even invited to the decision-making table, especially as more schools and school districts turn to for-profit corporations for their own management, curriculum materials, and assessment. Teachers are less able to organize and collectively negotiate to improve schools and their own working conditions, particularly in a culture that considers teachers and their organizations a "special interest," or where it has become acceptable to publicly demonize unions (as happened a few years ago when then–secretary of education Rod Paige called the National Education Association "terrorist"). Teachers are facing increasing restrictions in what and how to teach: initiatives in several states, for example, curtail curriculum in order to enforce a "teach to the test" regimen; other policies require teachers to act as

Focus point

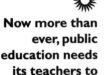

Now more than ever, public education needs its teachers to mobilize and act.

little more than mindless clerks following written scripts and dispensing predigested bits of curriculum into passive young people.

Teachers stand with students and parents at the center of school life; effective teachers must be thoughtful, caring people and oppose, then, any policy that encourages carelessness or thoughtlessness. Teachers' voices are absolutely vital to any efforts at positive and lasting school improvement. This is why the work of teachers today urgently involves changing education policy, and now more than ever, public education needs its teachers to mobilize and act.

THE POWER OF FRAMES

During the 2008 presidential campaign, conservative candidates said repeatedly that we must get the "lazy and incompetent teachers" out of public school classrooms, and who could disagree? Who would possibly stand up and insist that the lazy ones be promoted, or that "my kids deserve the incompetent"? Audiences dutifully and duly nodded on cue. Whichever politician made the point instantly won the point simply by framing the issue in that specific way: the terms were set, the options limited, and the verdict in.

But imagine if one of us had gotten to the podium first: we'd have said, "Every student in any public school classroom deserves an intellectually curious, morally grounded, thoughtful, caring, and compassionate teacher who is both well compensated and well rested." By framing the issue that way, we'd have gotten support, too. Setting the frame turns out to be a particularly powerful piece of work—who names the world, and who frames the issues, matters.

In area after area, issue after issue, we might productively open space for debate as we question and resist the wisdom of the dominant framework for discussion: why is our foreign policy based on military might rather than the principle of living together as a nation among nations? The issue is framed in what has become an orthodox dogma, something that appears to be just plain old common sense and therefore beyond question: national security depends on military power. But what is the actual evidence? What's the proof? Even asking the questions begins to open our eyes.

TEXTBOX 5.1

Why does every newspaper have a business section but not a labor section? Why is our notion of public safety based on escalating rates of incarceration? Why are workers who cross borders seeking jobs called "illegal immigrants" while capital that crosses borders seeking profit is never called "illegal money"? And why are the conditions that give rise to the movement of labor—collapsing prices and massive unemployment caused by the unchecked flow of capital and environmental degradation—rarely mentioned? The frame itself is a kind of insistent answer, a force that shapes our imaginative horizons and hence our choices.

Returning to education and schools, why is the so-called achievement gap accepted as an empirical reality decontextualized from the "education debt" (Ladson-Billings 1996) and "savage inequalities" (Kozol 1991), or absent a sustained critique of the testing industry?

The framework in which the discussion about schools and reform is carried forth is particularly narrow today; the dominant discourses and common metaphors are constraining and controlling. The frame includes, as noted earlier, a focus on *standards* for students, teachers, and schools developed by powerful interest groups but divorced from standards for legislatures, for example to generously fund education; *accountability* for reaching those standards as measured exclusively on anemic but widely accepted standardized test results and, again, without input by those directly affected and separated from any accountability whatsoever for lawmakers; and *sanctions* placed on schools and teachers for failing to meet those standards, combined with rewards for doing so.

These frames have been established over the past several decades, and today this framework constitutes a kind of consensus within the dominant political class. Although the 1994 reauthorization of the Elementary and Secondary Education Act during the Clinton administration required states to develop content and performance standards, and created the notion of "adequate yearly progress," it was the early years of the Reagan administration and the release of its report, *A Nation at Risk,* that signaled the beginning of a standards-and-testing movement that has dominated educational policy and politics for the past quarter century. Education reform has been framed by the language of standards and testing from both political parties, the dominant mass media, as well as in individual school districts across the nation. Chicago Public Schools, for example, influenced Clinton's vision of education reform in the mid-1990s by providing what he called "a model for the nation" in terms of standards, high-stakes testing, school accountability, and centralized regulation of teachers and schools. From both Republicans and Democrats, proposals for education reform have been shaped by the same concepts, thus reinforcing the notion that these are just naturally occurring phenomena, the only sensible way things can be; they achieve the lofty status of "common sense."

A consensus within the two dominant political parties does not mean that the standards-and-testing movement has proceeded without dissent. On the contrary, disagreement, protest, struggle, and dissent from teachers, parents, schools, and districts have marked the movement from the start. But the opposition has mainly struggled within the terms provided by the dominant frame—for more funding to get the test scores up, for example, or for different testing instruments—rather than organizing toward a new consensus based on a profoundly different educational vision.

In the contested space of schools and education reform, and in this particular moment, educators, parents, and citizens might find ways to rethink and challenge the dominant framework that has so relentlessly undermined the tenets of education in and for democracy. We might work together to upend the controlling metaphor that posits education as a commodity rather than a democratic and human right. We would reject, then, the notion that schools are just like little factories cranking out products, a failed nineteenth-century image for twenty-first-century schools. We would disrupt the language of production—assembly lines, management and supervision, quality control, productivity, and outputs—and of war—in the trenches, on the front lines. We would oppose the representation of students as raw materials moving dumbly down the assembly line as value is added by the workers/teachers.

In a democracy every life matters.

The schools-as-factories model is not only a failure on its own terms, but worse, it undermines the basic ideal that in a democracy every life matters. The goal of sorting kindergartners or seventh graders or high school kids into a track for winners and another track for losers is in basic conflict with the precious ideals of democratic living.

A foundational belief in the value of every human is belied by current "reform"—closing schools, privatizing the public space, testing children relentlessly. Michelle Rhee, the young Teach for America alumna and head of the Washington, D.C., schools, was featured in a cover story in *Time* magazine called "How to Fix America's Schools." Rhee is currently the chief executive officer, an honorific and official designation that has swept the nation—the business metaphor ascendant, knocking out the traditional and presumably lowly title of "superintendent of schools." In any case, the article turns on unrestrained praise for Rhee for making more changes in a year and a half on the job than other school leaders—"even reform-minded ones"—make in five: closing twenty-one schools (15 percent of schools in the district) and firing one hundred central office personnel, 270 teachers, and thirty-six principals. These are policy moves held on faith to stand for improvement, *but* they only make sense if education is a product like a stove or a box of bolts. Look at the list; this is downsizing and cost-cutting, the kinds of things we read about as General Motors emerges from bankruptcy. There is not one word in the *Time* piece about kids' learning or engagement with school, nothing about connecting curriculum to any idea of relevance or rigor; there isn't a nod to any evidence that might connect these "reform" moves with any measure of student progress. There's no mention of getting greater resources into this starving and depleted urban school system, an essential part of real reform. There are no ideas for more robust parent involvement, and no actions planned that might attract, reward, and retain terrific teachers for the long haul. So the heart of schooling is missing, the soul of it is absent, the wisdom nonexistent, and yet this, we are assured, is reform, and we're asked to accept it on faith. That is the power of frames.

This context provides all the more reason for educators to work to improve education policy. Progressive change happens not merely when a strong individual assumes a position of leadership but, much more important, when each one of us assumes the responsibility to lead, to take action, to build motion and a movement. Social justice in education is needed now. And every educator—at every grade level, in every subject area—has a role to play.

Social justice in education is needed now. And every educator—at every grade level, in every subject area—has a role to play.

THE POWER OF VOICE

Many educators in K–12 schools and in higher education have insightful critiques of current "reforms" and have imagined viable alternative policies and practices for our nation's public schools. Too often those critiques and alternative visions have remained within the confines of the teachers' lunchroom or small discussion groups or the ivory towers of higher education; only occasionally have they reached out to and involved a wider audience. To engage broadly in new ways of thinking and talking about public education, we all must do more to extend the public square, reframe the debate, and reclaim the public voice as we build toward a new movement in a committed, coordinated, and sustained way.

We need to speak up and speak out, using every available means to be heard and to have an impact. We can work with students in classrooms around educational issues, encouraging them to conduct their own critical action research projects and then helping them to procure public venues to present their work (see Youth Radio, for example: Jacinda Abcarian, jacinda@youthradio.org; or Lissa Soep, lissa@youthradio.org). Excellent classroom examples can be found at the Arts and Humanities Academy at Berkeley High School, where teachers and kids do quite a number of interesting investigations that are published or displayed. For example, they do an immigration unit that includes interviews and an art project—a portrait of an immigrant (contact Miriam Klein Stahl at cake3@mindspring.com).

We can seek out independent media outlets and shows, and we can produce content or build relationships around educational issues that may prove to be mutually productive (Democracy Now! radio and TV or Guerrilla News Network, for example). We can offer to contribute to more established shows such as *This American Life, This I Believe,* and *The Story,* all produced for National Public Radio and each actively soliciting story ideas. We can create our own media—blogs and vlogs and webinars; street theater and performance art (Google the Interventionists, Reverend Billy, or the Yes Men for breathtaking inspiration); poster art, broadsides, and mural displays (see AREA Chicago for one example of a sustained and extraordinary effort)—or we can partner

up and find space within existing blogs and more established networks (Huffington Post and Eduwonkette, for
example). We can access and utilize YouTube and Face-
book and other social networking groups. We can com-
ment publicly on legislation, and we can create our own
online petitions.

The essential thing is to start to speak and write regularly, to exercise your democratic responsibility to make
some noise in the public square, and to link up with
other teachers and education activists to make a plan to
make a difference.

One important and underutilized way to amplify the
voices of social justice educators and advocates is to
speak up in national and local newspapers throughout
the country. Although the media has historically privi-
leged the voices of the political and societal elite, local
TV and radio stations often have a designated space for
guest commentary, and newspaper editors almost always
reserve a section of the newspaper—typically the "op-ed"
page—for divergent opinions, including opinions that
challenge conventional wisdom. These editors are eager
for intelligent, well-argued contributions. According to
the Progressive Media Project (www.progressive
.org/mp/about), the op-ed section was created for the
open exchange of "new ideas and divergent opinions. . . .
[I]t is where the general public mulls over the arguments
about the way the world should be. It is also the place
where policy-makers measure the mood of the public
and gain new perspectives on social issues." Perhaps not
surprisingly, the editorial section of newspapers remains
one of the most commonly read sections following the
main and sports sections, with almost half of the general
readership looking at the editorials that are published in
their daily newspapers, according to the Newspaper Association of America (www.naa.org).

Editorials generally consist of four types of articles: (1)
"editorials" written by newspaper staff; (2) "columns"
written by regular contributors; (3) pieces written by
members of the community, variously called "commen-

tary," "opinion," or **"op-ed"** articles; and (4) "letters to the editor," written by members of the public. The latter two are important avenues for educators and advocates to reframe the debate on public education.

"Commentary" articles are generally five hundred words in length (longer in the major newspapers). They can take days or even weeks to be reviewed and accepted for publication. "Letters to the Editor" are generally much shorter, but are accepted by more newspapers, including online newspapers, and in greater numbers than commentary articles. Newspapers often prefer to publish articles and letters by members of the community in which the newspaper is published.

Every newspaper is different, so when getting started it's important to carefully read the instructions for submissions (regarding length, format, and review processes) as well as previous articles and letters (regarding recent topics, tone). Sample op-ed articles can be found on the website of the Progressive Media Project (www.progressive.org/mp/about).

CONCLUSION

We often meet brilliant young activists who choose not to go into teaching because they can't see how, in today's public schools, it would be possible to be an activist-educator. Among colleagues and friends and relatives who are veteran teachers, we see people leaving the profession for much the same reason. The challenges are daunting: the pressure to teach to the test, the narrowing and even scripting of curriculum, the increasing professional demands and public criticism, the heightened monitoring and censoring of anything or anyone deemed too "political" (that is, too willing to question the status quo or the powers that be), and the muting of teacher voices in school governance and education reform. Now more than ever, we need to redefine what it means to be a teacher, and activism must become a central part of that identity.

TEXTBOX 5.2

Although there are many ways to structure a compelling commentary, the following outline highlights elements that are common in published op-ed articles:

- The topic is timely; in other words, the article has a "news peg," a connection to something happening today.
- The first two sentences concisely state the subject and attitude of the essay—something like "Congress is poised to reauthorize many aspects of NCLB. This is bad news for America's children, because NCLB does not address three major problems with public schooling."
- The body of the commentary defends your position with two to four arguments—too many arguments makes the article complicated to follow—and for each argument provides compelling support, such as data or personal stories.
- The discussion rebuts the obvious counterarguments—it anticipates and responds to what a typical reader might ask.
- The conclusion is strong and does not introduce any new arguments.

Notice the following use of language in published commentaries and letters to the editor:

- Short paragraphs, short sentences, small words (the article needs to be easy to skim)
- Active tense ("the committee proposed a solution," rather than "a solution was proposed by the committee")
- No use of categoricals ("best," "always") or overheated language ("outrageous," "ridiculous") or of jargon (the article needs to be accessible, so avoid language like inflated academic terms that only a small group would understand)

When brainstorming an outline for your essay, consider the following six guiding questions:

continues

- WHEN are you writing? What is your news peg? (Right before the beginning of the school year? Impending state budget cuts? Election of a new U.S. president?)
- WHO/WHERE is your audience? (Are you writing for a national newspaper? Local newspaper? Ethnic newspaper? School newsletter? This helps to tailor the message and to imagine the obvious counterargument.)
- WHAT is your message? (Do you have a concise thesis statement?)
- HOW will you flesh out your message? (What are the two to four main arguments, and how is each argument being supported?)
- WHAT is the obvious counterargument, and have you rebutted it?
- WHY are you writing/what is your goal? (For example, what action do you hope will result? Do you want readers to speak to their legislators? Attend an upcoming rally? Vote against a referendum?)

The insights and experiences of teachers can play a central role in challenging the dominant voices in education debates. We encourage all teachers—those just entering the profession as well as those nearing the end of their careers—to join colleagues from throughout the nation in engaging public dialogue and reframing public consciousness. There are many ways to think about the problems and the possibilities of public education, and we need to hear perspectives that challenge what has come to be "common sense."

THREE SAMPLE OP-ED ARTICLES

In mid-December 2008, as preparations were under way for the start of the new administration, President-elect Barack Obama selected Arne Duncan, CEO of Chicago

Public Schools, to be the next U.S. secretary of education. In the days following, a number of media outlets lavished praise on this selection. One of us felt that we needed to offer a counterperspective, particularly given the significance of that historical moment. The spring of 2009 would be when the new president begins his term and sets the tone and priorities for his administration—what historians often look to as the "first hundred days." The spring of 2009 would also bring renewed efforts within Congress to reauthorize the Elementary and Secondary Education Act, and in the process, create opportunities to significantly change the problematic policies of No Child Left Behind. A shorter version of the following op-ed article was first published in the December 23, 2008, issue of the *Atlanta Journal-Constitution*. It was later published in its entirety in the January 12, 2009, online edition of *Education Week*.

Wrong Choice for America's Schools

Hailed by some as a pioneer in education reform, Arne Duncan was recently selected by President-elect Obama to be our next Secretary of Education. However, his track record as the CEO of Chicago Public Schools for the past seven years shows that Duncan is the wrong choice for America's schools.

Behind the rhetoric of "reform" is the reality of Duncan's accomplishments, particularly the problems behind his signature initiative, Renaissance 2010. Launched in 2004, Renaissance 2010 aims to open 100 new smaller schools (and close about sixty "failing" schools) by the year 2010. To date, seventy-five new schools have opened.

However, many of them are charter schools that serve fewer low-income, limited-English-proficient and disabled students than regular public schools. More than a third of them are in communities that are not high-needs areas. During Duncan's tenure, district-wide high school test scores have not risen, and most of the lowest performing high schools saw scores drop. Renaissance 2010 is not doing enough to support those students who struggle the most.

This should not be surprising. The blueprint of Renaissance 2010 lies in a report titled "Left Behind," produced a year earlier by the Commercial Club of Chicago, which mapped out a strategy for schools to more closely align with the goals of the business elite. Central to that strategy was the creation of 100 new charter schools, managed by for-profit businesses, and freed of Local School Councils and teacher unions—groups that historically have put the welfare of poor and minority students before that of the business sector.

Business leaders have long had influence over America's schools. In the early 1900s, the business sector influenced how large school districts were consolidated and managed. In the late 1900s and into the era of No Child Left Behind, the Business Roundtable (the top 300 business CEOs in America) influenced how policy makers narrowly defined "standards" and "accountability." Today, public debates are framed by business principles, and certain assumptions go unquestioned and are seen to be "common sense." This includes the assumption that improvement comes when schools are put into competition with one another, like businesses in a so-called free market.

Duncan's reforms are steeped in a free-market model of school reform, particularly the notion that school choice and 100 new charter and specialty schools will motivate educators to work harder to do better (as will penalties for not meeting standards). But research does not support such initiatives. There is evidence that opening new schools and encouraging choice and competition will not raise district-wide achievement, and charter schools in particular are not outperforming regular schools. There is evidence that choice programs actually exacerbate racial segregation. And there is evidence that high-stakes testing actually increases the dropout rate.

Duncan's track record is clear. Less court intervention to desegregate schools. Less parental and community involvement in school governance. Less support for teacher unions. Less breadth and depth in what and how students learn as schools place more emphasis on narrow high-stakes testing. More opportunities to certify teachers without adequate preparation and training. More penalties for schools but without adequate resources for those in high-poverty areas. And more profit for businesses as school systems become increasingly privatized. Students do not benefit from these changes. Duncan's accomplishments for Chicago Public Schools are not a model for the nation.

America's schools are in dire need of reform, and in 2009, we have the opportunity to overhaul the failed policies of No Child Left Behind. The research is compelling: students need to learn more, not less. Parents need to be involved more, not less. Teachers need to be trained more. Schools need to be resourced more. We need new ways to fund schools, to integrate schools, to evaluate learning, and to envision what we want schools to accomplish.

Public education should aim for more than high test scores, and more than a stronger business sector. Education should strive to prepare every child to flourish in life. We need a different leader, one with a rich knowledge of research, with a commitment to educating our diverse children, and with a vision to make that happen.

At the same time, another one of us published a different perspective on the new secretary of education, and what this selection means for us as advocates of public education. The following op-ed appeared on the Huffington Post on January 2, 2009.

Obama and Education Reform

Of course I would have loved to have seen Linda Darling-Hammond become Secretary of Education in an Obama administration. She's smart, honest, compassionate and courageous, and perhaps most striking, she actually knows schools and classrooms, curriculum and teaching, kids and child development. These have never counted for much as qualifications for the post, of course, and yet they offer a neat contrast with the four failed urban school superintendents—Michelle Rhee, Joel Klein, Paul Vallas, and Arne Duncan—who were for weeks rumored to be her chief competition.

These four, like George W. Bush's Secretary of Education, Rod Paige of the fraudulent Texas-miracle, have little to show in terms of school improvement beyond a deeply dishonest public relations narrative. Teacher accountability, relentless standardized testing, school closings, and privatization—this is what the dogmatists and true-believers of the right call "reform." Michelle Rhee of Washington, D.C., the most ideologically driven of the bunch, warranted a cover story in *Time* in early December called "How to Fix America's Schools," in which she was praised for making more changes in a year and a half on the job than other school leaders, "even reform-minded ones," make in five: closing 21 schools (15 percent of the total), firing 100 central office personnel, 270 teachers, and 36 principals. These are all policy moves that are held on faith to stand for improvement; not a word on kids' learning or engagement with schools, not even a nod at evidence that might connect these moves with student progress. But of course evidence is always the enemy of dogma, and this is faith-based, fact-free school policy at its purest.

So I would have picked Darling-Hammond, but then again I would have picked Noam Chomsky for state, Naomi Klein for defense, Bernardine Dohrn for Attorney General, Bill Fletcher for commerce, James Thindwa for labor, Barbara Ransby for human services, Paul Krugman for treasury, and Amy Goodman for press secretary. So what do I know?

Darling-Hammond would not have been a smart pick for Obama. She was steadily demonized in a concerted campaign to undermine her effectiveness, and she would

surely have had great difficulty getting any traction whatsoever for progressive policy change in this environment.
Arne Duncan was the smart choice, the unity choice—
the least driven by ideology, the most open to working
with teachers and unions, the smartest by a mile—and
let's wish him well.

But there's a deeper point: since the Obama victory,
many people seem to be suffering a kind of post-partum
depression: unable to find any polls to obsess over, we
read the tea-leaves and try to penetrate the president-
elect's mind. What do his moves portend? What magic
or disaster awaits us? With due respect, this is a matter of
looking entirely in the wrong direction.

Obama is not a monarch—Arne Duncan is not education czar—and we are not his subjects. If we want a
foreign policy based on justice, for example, we ought to
get busy organizing a robust anti-imperialist peace movement; if we want to end the death penalty we better get
smart about changing the dominant narrative concerning crime and punishment. We are not allowed to sit
quietly in a democracy awaiting salvation from above.
We are all equal, and we all need to speak up and speak
out right now.

During Arne Duncan's tenure in Chicago, a group of
hunger-striking mothers organized city-wide support
and won the construction of a new high school in a community that had been underserved and denied for years.
Another group of parents, teachers, and students mobilized to push military recruiters out of their high school;
Duncan didn't support them and he certainly didn't lead
the charge, but they won anyway. If they'd waited for
Duncan to act, they'd likely be waiting still. Teachers at
another school refused to give one of the endless standardized tests, arguing that this was one test too many,
and they organized deep support for their protest; Duncan didn't support them either, but they won anyway. If
they'd waited for Duncan, they'd be waiting still. Why
would anyone sit around waiting for Arne now? Stop

whining; get busy. In the realm of education, there is nothing preventing any of us from pressing to change the dominant discourse that has controlled the discussion for many years. It's reasonable to assume that education in a democracy is distinct from education under a dictatorship or a monarchy, but how? Surely school leaders in fascist Germany or communist Albania or medieval Saudi Arabia all agreed, for example, that students should behave well, stay away from drugs and crime, do their homework, study hard, and master the subject matters, so those things don't differentiate a democratic education from any other.

What makes education in a democracy distinct is a commitment to a particularly precious and fragile ideal, and that is a belief that the fullest development of all is the necessary condition for the full development of each; conversely, the fullest development of each is necessary for the full development of all.

Democracy, after all, is geared toward participation and engagement, and it's based on a common faith: every human being is of infinite and incalculable value, each a unique intellectual, emotional, physical, spiritual, and creative force. Every human being is born free and equal in dignity and rights; each is endowed with reason and conscience, and deserves, then, a sense of solidarity, brotherhood and sisterhood, recognition and respect.

We want our students to be able to think for themselves, to make judgments based on evidence and argument, to develop minds of their own. We want them to ask fundamental questions—who in the world am I? How did I get here and where am I going? What in the world are my choices? How in the world shall I proceed?—and to pursue answers wherever they might take them. Democratic educators focus their efforts, not on the production of things so much as on the production of fully developed human beings who are capable of controlling and transforming their own lives, citizens who can participate fully in civic life.

Democratic teaching encourages students to develop initiative and imagination, the capacity to name the world, to identify the obstacles to their full humanity, and the courage to act upon whatever the known demands. Education in a democracy should be characteristically eye-popping and mind-blowing—always about opening doors and opening minds as students forge their own pathways into a wider world.

How do our schools here and now measure up to the democratic ideal?

Much of what we call schooling forecloses or shuts down or walls off meaningful choice-making. Much of it is based on obedience and conformity, the hallmarks of every authoritarian regime. Much of it banishes the unpopular, squirms in the presence of the unorthodox, hides the unpleasant. There's no space for skepticism, irreverence, or even doubt. While many of us long for teaching as something transcendent and powerful, we find ourselves too often locked in situations that reduce teaching to a kind of glorified clerking, passing along a curriculum of received wisdom and predigested and often false bits of information. This is a recipe for disaster in the long run.

Educators, students, and citizens must press now for an education worthy of a democracy, including an end to sorting people into winners and losers through expensive standardized tests which act as pseudo-scientific forms of surveillance; an end to starving schools of needed resources and then blaming teachers and their unions for dismal outcomes; and an end to the rapidly accumulating "educational debt," the resources due to communities historically segregated, under-funded and under-served. All children and youth in a democracy, regardless of economic circumstance, deserve full access to richly resourced classrooms led by caring, qualified and generously compensated teachers. So let's push for that, and let's make it happen before Arne Duncan or anyone else grants us permission.

The following month, two of us published an op-ed in one of the local Chicago newspapers about the intersection of militarizing public schools and discriminating against lesbian, gay, bisexual, and transgender individuals. The following article was published in the *Windy City Times* on February 25, 2009.

Queer Eyes on What Prize?
Ending Don't Ask, Don't Tell

So, we've heard that Barack Obama is going to repeal the *Don't Ask, Don't Tell* policy that prohibits gays and lesbians from serving openly in the military. As two queer teachers that have been working hard to arrest the militarism of education in Chicago—a public high school for every branch of the military, and two for the army (and not one of these with a Gay Straight Alliance for students), and over 10,000 youth from 6th to 12th grade participating in some form of military program in their public schools—we are not leaping with joy at this rumor. Our reluctance has our allies scratching their heads:

"Isn't this what you want?"

"Equal right to fight!"

"What a success for the gay rights movement!"

"I guess this solves the discrimination problem in military public schools, then."

"Gay kids can join up!"

Sure, we think uniforms are hot, but this—permitting out lesbians and gay men to enlist—was never the purpose of gay liberation, a movement aiming as tenaciously at peace as equal rights.

And for us, it's clear that overturning *Don't Ask, Don't Tell* (DADT) won't begin to address the public policy catastrophe of turning over our public schools, and some of our nation's poorest youth, to the military.

We argue that the system of public education should remain a civilian system. This statement rests on three proposals. First, adults may choose to enlist; youth cannot. Next, schools should educate students for the broadest possibilities and choices; the military narrowly aims to prepare recruits. And last, schools should protect young people and nurture peace; but the military is contagiously violent. From the ugly revelations of Abu Ghraib, and the rash of sexual assaults on military women by men in service, to many veterans' post-service violence turned both inward and outward—its legacy of brutality is so vast that the Department of Defense might more aptly be called the Department of Destruction.

This proposed repeal, far from any big win, offers queers an important opportunity to think about our strategies and goals. Let's not unfurl our victory banner too quickly; instead, we should keep our queer eyes, and organizing, focused on the real prize: social justice.

Yes, gays, lesbians, and transgendered folks are discriminated against and excluded from full participation in our society and its institutions, including schools (read any report about rates of violence against gay students or employment discrimination for out queer or non-gender conforming school staff), military (DADT—enough said?), families (remember the 57 percent majority that passed the 2008 gay adoption ban in Arkansas), and religion (many religious colleges and universities ban homosexual students, staff, and faculty—legally!).

Add to this list the ease with which otherwise smart people, including President Obama, reserve marriage and all its attendant privileges for "one man and one woman" while also claiming they are "ferocious" defenders of gay rights—that's a fairly self-serving stance, isn't it? Yes, gays and lesbians still have a long way to go toward achieving . . . let's just call it "fully human status" in the United States.

The push to repeal DADT is, on the one hand, a no-brainer—all people should have all rights, right?

But this proposal can also be understood, and it is by us, as an attempt to remap what our social justice goals, as queers, should be—not the right to privacy and the right to public life, and certainly not the right to live lives free from our nation's ever-present militarism and never-ending war. Instead, lesbians, gays, transgendered, and bisexuals are encouraged to forget our historical places at the helm of social justice thinking and labor (to mention just a few, Jane Addams, Bayard Rustin, Barbara Jordan, and of course, Harvey Milk), constrict our vision and dreams, and just be happy for an opportunity to participate in a military that depends on poverty and permanent war to keep enlistment high.

Let's forget repealing DADT and cut right to the chase: Repeal the Department of Defense. What about establishing a Department of Peace, as Dennis Kucinich has already proposed? Let's pair that with bear brigades tossing pink batons (and, of course, an annual teddy bear picnic). Or, we can take up the mermaid parade as an organizing celebration, with its dress-up and float creation. Either of these fanciful, and very queer, forms would allow us all to play and create together, and each seems a better activity for a school to take up than pretend soldiering.

Then let's organize for some real social justice goals.

For starters, let's demand universal healthcare, affordable housing, and meaningful living wage employment that supports flourishing, not merely subsisting, lives, for all.

We know we don't need 6th or 12th graders wearing military uniforms, marching with wooden guns on public school grounds. We don't need twelve-year-olds parsing military ranks or plotting battles. However, we could use more teens painting murals, stitching gowns, and writing code and lyrics. In short, we don't need child soldiers, but we could use more young artists.

A public school system that teaches peace and art, with fiercely equal opportunities for all students. We can see it now: painting classes, soccer clubs, computer gaming classes, drum kits, comprehensive sexuality education, and musical theater in every school. That's so excellently queer, and so very just.

DISCUSSION QUESTIONS

1. What are some ways that the media and popular culture have represented what it means to be a teacher? What are some images that come to mind? How do these compare with your own experiences in school?

2. If you had the opportunity to meet with the U.S. secretary of education, or the superintendent of your local school district, what are the top five problems in education that you would want to discuss, and why?

3. What is an issue in education that you believe needs to be reframed? Using the "six guiding questions," draft an outline for an op-ed article in which you present a new way of seeing the issue. Consider submitting your article to a local newspaper!

FURTHER READING

Lakoff, George. 2004. *Don't Think of an Elephant: Know Your Values and Frame the Debate.* New York: Chelsea Green.
An eye-opening description of the power of frames in political campaigns and elections.
Shaker, Paul, and Elizabeth E. Heilman. 2008. *Reclaiming Education for Democracy: Thinking Beyond No Child Left Behind.* New York: Routledge.
An analysis of frames in current federal legislation.

ALSO OF INTEREST

Hijacking Catastrophe, a documentary film by the Media Education Foundation about the strategic ways that war and safety have been framed in the United States; and *Sicko,* a documentary film by Michael Moore about the strategic ways that health care has been framed in the United States.

AFTERWORD

THE CHICAGO POET Gwendolyn Brooks wrote a praise song to the dazzling freedom fighter and Renaissance man Paul Robeson, a man who loved music and the arts, a man who knew the elegance of mathematics and espoused the scientific method, a black man in America who fiercely embraced all of humanity and tried to make that embrace have a concrete and vital meaning in the muck and the mud of the real world as he found it: Brooks describes a clear and powerful voice "cutting across the hot grit of the day." A major voice, she asserts, the mature adult voice, deep and resonant, "Warning, in music words / devout and large, / that we are each other's harvest: / we are each other's / business: /we are each other's / magnitude and bond."

As teachers we engage in a front-end effort for a more human world—"we are each other's business," "we are each other's magnitude and bond"—a world based on the as-yet-unrealized ideal that every person's life is of infinite value. We resist, then, all the constructed hierarchies of human worth and worthlessness as base and ugly—wrong in the sense of inaccurate, and wrong in the sense of immoral.

Our stance as teachers of and for democracy is identification *with* our students and communities, not identification *of*—the latter moves dangerously toward surveillance. And we struggle as Jane Addams, another Chicago visionary, struggled to hold to the idea of the unity of humanity, even—or perhaps especially—when humanity is represented by a delinquent boy, an alcoholic woman, a drug-addicted teenager, or a gangbanger. The unity of humanity: the development of all is the baseline for the development of each. And so we reaffirm a commitment to education as a search for enlightenment and liberation, education as the practice of freedom, education as humanization. *Humanization refers to the process of becoming more intentional and more powerful in creating a world where more people more of the time act as sisters and brothers toward one another.*

Focus point

We reject and oppose, then, any action that treats anyone else as an object, any gesture that objectifies or *thingifies* human beings. We insist that our classrooms pivot on the recognition of the humanity of each person who shares that space: students, teachers, families, guests. "The starting point of critical elaboration is the consciousness of what one really is," Antonio Gramsci wrote in his *Prison Notebooks*, "and is 'knowing thyself' as a product of the historical process to date, which has deposited in you an infinity of traces, without leaving an inventory." Gramsci articulates a sense of the infinite and the ineffable tied up inexorably with the concrete and the real. We are made of the traces from each and all—and from the facts of nature and the sweep of culture and history—but we can never be finally summarized. We are always more, always arcing forward, always a site of potential and possibility.

We gear our efforts to helping every human being reach a fuller measure of his or her humanity.

This belief in the preciousness and the infinite value of every human being shapes our work as teachers and as citizens of a democracy. It insists that we gear our efforts to helping every human being reach a fuller measure of his or her humanity. It invites people on an immense and ongoing journey to become more thoughtful and more

capable, more powerful and courageous, more exquisitely alive in their projects and their pursuits. An unyielding belief in the unity of humanity—always
revolutionary, and never more so than today—is never
quite finished, never easily or adequately summed up,
and yet it is central to achieving both a decent classroom
and a just society. Neither a commodity with readily recognized features nor a product for consumption, the
democratic ideal is an aspiration to be continually nourished, engaged, and exercised, a dynamic, expansive experiment that must be approached and achieved over
and over again by every individual and each successive
generation if it is to live at all.

**This
fundamental
commitment—
the solidarity of
humanity—is a
principle easier
to articulate
than to live out
on the ground.**

This fundamental commitment—the solidarity of
humanity—is a principle easier to articulate than to live
out on the ground, easier to uphold as a slogan than to
enact in the real classrooms, schools, and communities
we actually inhabit. To take one complicating example:
we embrace stories like Helen Keller's, books like *The
Miracle Worker*, *My Left Foot*, and *Under the Eye of the
Clock*. Each is a story of overcoming adversity, each the
tale of a teacher who recognized inside a broken or disabled body a human spark to nourish and encourage and
blow into a blazing flame of triumph and redemption.
Beautiful. Moving. Inspirational. Wildly popular in our
culture.

And yet we can't help noticing that the families of
these youngsters had advantages and privileges, access
and means and social power to intervene in tough circumstances and to fight against seemingly unyielding
systems. Nor can we deny the casual disregard of the humanity of thousands and thousands—millions really—of
young people, including the students many of us work
with and worry about every day, who made the mistake
of being born poor, for example, who hold no currency,
have limited access and little recognition. The inspirational stories, then, remain bright baubles, Hallmark
cards and romantic turns rather than calls to arms.

We work every day so that our students might become seekers after their own questions, authors of their own scripts.

Those of us who work with young people whose humanity is routinely tossed aside see dehumanization as both policy and practice, and yet we desperately want for our young people those miracles and transformations, those hard efforts, enduring hopes, and generous investments. This is the territory of our determined efforts for a more decent and humane, a more balanced and human, world. We work every day so that our students might become seekers after their own questions, authors of their own scripts and not bit players in stories already written for them by others, actors in their own dramas, artists and composers of their own lives. We are ever mindful of the young man's outburst in Gwendolyn Brooks's "Boy Breaking Glass": "I shall create!" he cries. "If not a note / a hole. If not an overture / a desecration." But I shall create.

Children and youth desperately seek a sense of their place in the universe. Everyone needs to be recognized, everyone wants to be special and distinct, and everyone wants to leave a footprint in the sand: I am here; I am somebody. Like all human beings, students want to know that they are valuable and valued, that they can be of use. If they are always treated as "objects" and taught "subjects," they will be pushed away from their deepest hopes and their greatest promise.

Teachers who understand the unique capacity of human beings to shape and create reality through conscious purposes and deliberate plans are poised to transform their classrooms into sites that provide children with ongoing opportunities to exercise that latent resourcefulness: to solve real problems in their real communities, to act, to change, to make a difference.

We work with our students to embody the change we want to see in the world. We show them (and ourselves) what it means in practice to live purposefully, honestly, ethically, fully. We can't wait passively for someone else—the school board, the state legislature, the union, the principal, the federal government—to get it right about teaching and schooling, about citizenship and learning to live together, about engagement and social responsibility, before we ourselves get it right in this corner of this specific classroom. We will all become more powerfully engaged if and when our hearts and hands are working to improve our daily lives and surroundings. We must change ourselves in order to be worthy of the larger changes that we long for—a world of peace, kindness, love, and justice. That world just might become an apt description of your classroom.

Our greatest failings as teachers come when we lose sight of any alternatives. Our imaginations become diminished or shut down. We settle too easily, then, for working in small, somewhat barricaded, and defensive positions. This is not good enough.

"All's well," says the town crier as he makes his rounds through the village, lighting the lamps for the night. The activist responds, "No, all is not well." This current moment is neither inevitable nor stable, and its imperfections—the unnecessary suffering, the undeserved pain—are cause for alarm. Our situations are neither fixed nor entirely determined; we are still in motion, still artists in residence and works in progress. History has not stood still for us; another world is both possible and inevitable: Get up! Get moving! Activists resist passivity and cynicism, and they announce the seeds of a world in the making. Let's create—right here and right now, in this community or in this school or in this corner of this classroom—a bit of the world we want to inhabit.

Teachers often feel themselves shackled, bound, and gagged, and yet here, too, another world is possible. Teachers might begin by noticing things as they are—if we want to ease the pain of living for ourselves, for our students and families, for our communities, we will need to pinch ourselves awake and blink our eyes open, not once or twice, but every day. It won't be easy because we must then confront the horrors. How should we act? What is to be done? We stir ourselves, a bit uncertainly perhaps,

Focus point

but we then take a step forward. It must feel awkward
and shaky. We take another step. And another.

We can, of course, choose to keep our eyes firmly shut
against injustice. We may not be able to claim much in
terms of moral action, but our lives would at least assume
the pretense of calm. We might also choose to anesthetize
ourselves with bread and circuses, get drunk on overcon-
sumption, and live out a puppet show of a simple existence. After all, as the great philosophers remind us, the
unexamined life may not be worth living, but the examined life is marked with anguish. On the other side, we
might open to the powerful and extreme feelings of a life
intensely lived: the ecstasy and the agony, joy exquisitely
balanced with suffering and pain. We may try with others
to forge ourselves into artisans of a new humanity. What
might that entail? What are our wildest dreams?

We need to make a distinction here between personal
virtues—be honest, do your work, and show up on
time—and democratic or community ethics. Personal
virtue is an undisputed good, but we would be hard-
pressed to say a slave owner who paid his bills on time
and was loyal or kind to his wife was an ethical person.
We need to think about how we act collectively, how our
society behaves, how the contexts of politics and econom-
ics, for example, interact with what we hold to be good.
Most of us, after all, most of the time follow the conven-
tions of our cultures—most Spartans act like Spartans;
most Athenians, like Athenians; most Americans, like
Americans—and, of course, most teachers act like teachers. To be a person of moral character in an unjust social
order (or even an imperfect democracy) requires something more: to work to change the society (or, say, the
school), to rewrite the narrative, to resist, and to invent.

Good teaching is always in search of better teaching,
and good teaching has a hard time finding adequate light
or air in a bad system. Just like the dilemma of living a
good life or being a good person in a slave society, becoming a good teacher demands that we open our eyes to

the larger system, that we identify obstacles and challenges to the full development of all, and that we work to change and improve that system for the benefit of everyone. The point, then, is not to search out a putatively perfect school where you can live happily ever after, but rather to recognize that part of your job as a teacher is to work to change the system in which your classroom, your students, and your teaching struggle to live.

Martin Luther King Jr. was an activist and a visionary performance artist who illuminated pieces of truth to vast audiences again and again, and demonstrated along the way the power of activism to generate courage, disrupt injustice, and posit alternatives to the status quo. Dr. King was an activist for only thirteen years, yet he grew and changed and deepened and developed every hour of every day of that journey. He fought ignorance and violence and injustice with love and direct action.

King was a notorious lawbreaker. He noted that some laws are just; traffic laws, for example, can be reasonable and fair. But even here, he pointed to the exceptions: a fire truck in a hurry to put out a fire is allowed to speed through stop signs, and an ambulance carrying a person bleeding to death can go right through the red light.

We need brigades of ambulance drivers today willing to drive through those red lights at top speed on behalf of a bleeding humanity, on behalf of children and families. We push hard to keep our democratic dreams alive: for example, we want to push for an urban/rural federal school bailout fund, a "Septima Clark Teacher Corps" to bring parents and unemployed folks into the schools as aids and teacher candidates, a peer restorative justice program in every school, an end to privatizing the public space, and the creation of a vast, messy, democratic community assembly to draw on the wisdom of everyone to rethink and renew curriculum and teaching.

In *Hard Times*, Charles Dickens introduces the schoolmaster in a chapter aptly titled "The Murder of Innocents"; it's a kind of meditation on the danger of imagination, choice, and free will to the people who are drunk on power, or the men of facts without ethics, or those cynics who can tell you the price of everything but the value of nothing. Dickens shows us the degradation and fear that mark the classroom as slave galley, where the teacher's central task is merely to beat the drum. Dickens himself turns at last to the schoolmaster with an indictment: "When . . . thou shalt fill each jar brim full by-and-by, dost thou think that thou wilt always kill outright the robber Fancy lurking within—or sometimes only maim him and distort him!"

Because we want to live in a more fully human world, a world of mutual recognition, we want to develop a richer and deeper vision of democracy, and a pedagogy of democracy as well. A pedagogy of engagement with and activism for humanity—something that tries to tell the truth; tries to stand against violence, war, exploitation, and oppression; and tries to act in fairness and balance and peace. A pedagogy that tries to enact the power of love that does justice.

SUGGESTED RESOURCES

Class Dismissed. France. A film about the boredom, isolation, irrelevance, and violence of education in the colonial mode.

Do the Right Thing. United States. A film about life on one city street on one hot day.

Not One Less. China. A film about an intrepid novice teacher going the distance to help one errant student.

Rabbit-Proof Fence. Australia. A film about schooling as a weapon of control, and the inevitable resistance from below.

To Have and to Be. France. A documentary about the wisdom and joys of teaching from a rural one-room schoolhouse.

INDEX

ABOUT THE AUTHORS

William Ayers is Distinguished Professor of Education at the University of Illinois at Chicago. His recent publications include *Race Course Against White Supremacy* (with Bernadine Dohrn) and the *Handbook of Social Justice in Education* (with Therese Quinn and David Stovall).

Kevin K. Kumashiro is Professor and Chair of Educational Policy Studies at the University of Illinois at Chicago and the founding director of the Center for Anti-Oppressive Education. His recent books include *The Seduction of Common Sense: How the Right Has Framed the Debate on America's Schools* and *Against Common Sense: Teaching and Learning Toward Social Justice.*

Erica R. Meiners is Professor of Education and Women's Studies at Northeastern Illinois University. She is the author of *Right to Be Hostile: Schools, Prisons, and the Making of Public Enemies,* and with Therese Quinn, *Flaunting It! Queers Organizing for Public Education and Justice,* and "Never Innocent: Feminist Trouble with Sex Offender Registries and Protection in a Prison Nation," in *Meridians: Feminism, Race, Transnationalism.*

Therese Quinn is Associate Professor of Art Education at the School of the Art Institute of Chicago. Her recent publications include *Flaunting*

It! Queers Organizing for Public Education and Justice and the *Handbook of Social Justice in Education.*

David Stovall is Associate Professor of Educational Policy Studies at the University of Illinois at Chicago. He is author of numerous scholarly and popular articles, poems, polemics, and reviews, and an editor of the *Handbook of Social Justice in Education.*